Business Essentials

By Hendrith Vanlon Smith Jr
CEO of Mayflower-Plymouth

Business Essentials
Contents first written 2015-2021
4th Edition, 2022
Hendrith Vanlon Smith Jr

ISBN: 978-1-387-89062-0
© 2022 Mayflower-Plymouth Capital LLC
© 2022 Hendrith Vanlon Smith Jr
© 2022 Chaya Ari Smith

Published by Mayflower-Plymouth

Copies held in the United States Copyright Office
Copies held in the Copyright Office of The Republic of Panama

Business Essentials
Hendrith Vanlon Smith Jr | *Mayflower-Plymouth*

Authors Introduction :

Business Essentials contains the fundamental principles of business success. It has purely refined bits of business wisdom to help every businessperson or entrepreneur to achieve lasting success, growth and fulfillment. The keys to success in business are contained in these pages. Studying this book will help you to be a better business person, a better leader, and a better manager. Consequently, the business you lead will experience growth, great profits, and phenomenal success.

This book is intended to provide quick bits of business wisdom that owners, managers, executives, entrepreneurs and employees can refer to on their path to greater business success. There are no scientific methodologies or exhaustive detailed data points. There are no statistics or graphs or charts. This isn't an MBA textbook. It's meant to be simple and to the point such that only the core essence of business is being expressed - nothing more. As the title implies, it's about the essentials of business. There's power in simplicity.

At Mayflower-Plymouth, we're passionate about helping businesses to accomplish their strategic goals and thrive. Our motto is 'Modelling Nature to thrive in Business.' This book is intended to help in that effort. Enjoy.

Essence:

Business is about putting smiles on peoples faces. Business is about helping people to live better lives.

A little bit more:

A business is a platform for giving customers and clients the products and services that they want or need. When they get the things they want and need, they're happy. When it's a good deal, they're glad to pay because the product or service they're getting means more to them at that moment than the money/currency they used to pay for it. So when you think about it this way, every business is kind of selling happiness and smiles- or at least some kind of satisfaction. Any exception to this rule is probably a kind of business that most people would vote to eliminate if they could.

Essence:

Businesses and markets have a symbiotic relationship. Each has a profound effect on the other.

A little bit more:

Each business is like a tree in a forest that is the economy/market. Each business is like a living being that exists within an ecosystem that also has a life of its own. What each tree does is important to the forest and what happens to the forest is important to each tree within that forest. It's the same kind of thing with businesses and markets.

Essence:

There's so much beauty in getting paid to do what you love. That should be at the heart of every business - people getting paid to do what they love.

A little bit more:

What each of us does for a living should be linked to our sense of purpose and our sense of fulfillment. When this is the case, we work harder and we work smarter and we really pour ourselves I to the work because it doesn't feel like work - we enjoy it. And when we get paid for this it's extremely satisfying. Imagine if all the jobs everywhere were filled by people who genuinely loved doing that job! It would be a wonderful world!

Essence:

Everything in this world has a business side to it.

A little bit more:

As an entrepreneur, you have to be able to look around and see everything from a business perspective. This will allow you to come up with better ideas and better solutions in business. When you're in the grocery store and see that for example the price of toothpaste has gone up while everything else seems price stable, ask yourself why. Maybe the laboratory company that makes the ingredients in the toothpaste has gone bankrupt. Maybe one of the key ingredients happens to come from a country that our government recently sanctioned. Or whatever. Maybe that means you should invest in the competitor laboratory company. Or, if sanctions look like they're going to stay a while, maybe you start a new business that becomes a supplier to major toothpaste brands.

Essence:

Business is about creating value for a specific group of people.

A little bit more:

It's not about trying to please everyone. It's not about trying to make everyone happy. It's not about solving everyone's problems. For each business, it's about operating in service to a specific group of people; a specific market. A company may have several lines of business each service a different group of people. So while the companysy have a variety of different kinds of customers, if you look closer you'll see a collection of smaller businesses each serving a specific group of people.

Essence:

If you want to have a profitable business, you need to have an efficient business. In business, efficiency is a prerequisite to profit.

A little bit more:

Efficiency is mandatory. When we look at nature, we see efficiency everywhere and we efficiency is it's systems. The way to get to profits is by having a system where revenues exceed costs. And the way to do that is to be efficient.

Business Efficiency has so many benefits. It leads to greater profits, greater internal leverage, less friction..... but it also leads to less waste, less pollution, and a richer harmony with nature

When a business streamlines its processes, it inevitably experiences other benefits which may include greater employee satisfaction, more profits, better accounting, and more.

Essence:

A good business adapts it's strategy and approach as the economy continuously evolves.

A little bit more:

The economy is always changing. So your business should always be changing. Managing a business includes adapting to change, evolving with change and sometimes pioneering those changes and evolutions.

A business is like a living being. It's more of a process than a stagnant thing. The way you manage your business today shouldn't be the same way you managed it ten years ago or even ten months ago. Because your business should have evolved and changed and adapted in some way during that time - just like living beings evolve and change and adapt to their environments.

Essence:

Every problem that we have in society has a suite of relative solutions that are also

business opportunities.

A little bit more:

Agricultural waste is a problem. But solving that problem is a business opportunity.

Energy inefficiency is a problem. But solving that problem is a business opportunity.

The abusive treatment of animals is a problem. But solving that problem is a business

opportunity. Reduced biodiversity is a problem. But solving that problem is a business

opportunity. Plastic waste in the ocean is a problem. But solving that problem is a

business opportunity. And the list goes on indefinitely. We just have to think creatively

and fluidly and we can solve all of these problems that plague Earth and we can grow

businesses and earn money and provide for our families in the process.

Essence:

People like to know that the companies they interact with and buy from are companies that do good in the world

A little bit more:

In business, brand is important and reputation is important. You want your business to actually be good and do good by aligning itself with scertain values and morals. And you want your business to also be perceived as good.

Essence:

To succeed in business, you've gotta understand your customers.

A little bit more:

The customers are the ones buying your products and services. You simply cannot succeed unless you understand them. You need to understand their motives, their desires, their demographics, their psychological nature and more. The better you understand your customers, the better you can serve them in exchange for profit.

Essence:

Productivity is about turning valuable inputs into valuable outputs. Individual people are more productive when all the elements of the permaculture economy are at work in their lives. When individuals are productive, then businesses become productive. When businesses become productive, the nation becomes productive.

A little bit more:

Every tree in every forest strives to be productive. They strive to do more with less. They strive to create an abundance. All of the businesses in the Mayflower-Plymouth ecosystem should strive to be productive in the same way. And all businesses everywhere.

Essence:

Nature isn't transactional. Nature is is about relationships and processes and systems. Transactions happen, but they happen within the clear context of relationships, processes and systems. Business should be like that. Markets should be like that. The economy should be like that.

A little bit more:

Observe a forest. You'll see lots of relationships at play. For example, the symbiotic relationship between the trees and the mycorrhizae. The mycorrhizae help the trees to communicate and share nutrients and information. The trees provide the mycorrhizae with mass. The relationship between the bees and the flowering plants in another example.

Essence:

Ass society evolves, business models evolve.

A little bit more:

Business models evolve along with the evolution of society. And often times it's the other way around and business models lead the evolution of society. It's a dance where each participant moves in harmony with the other, and in order to maintain sync, certain limitations are established.

Essence:

The basic and most fundamental element to business is creating value - creating value for others and making their lives better in some way. If you can do that, put a price on it, communicate it clearly and get it to buyers..... you're in business.

A little bit more:

It doesn't get more basic than this. Everyone is searching for value. Everyone's goal is to get more value and they're all willing to pay for that added value to varying degrees at varying times. The goal of the business is to provide that value.

Essence:

The profit motive is the most potent source of collective motivation and the most efficient means for society to solve its problems.

A little bit more:

Profit is the primary economic motivation in business and in an economy. Anywhere you insert a profit motive - people will self assemble groups, leverage resources, and implement processes all in the effort to satisfy that profit motive.

MORE

1. Business models are about the systems and processes related to the exchange of value between sellers and buyers.

2. Every business should be thinking about their flywheel and the way that value is upcycled internally.

3. The economy is always changing. Therefore, business strategy should change to adapt. And the way to adapt is to find new ways to add value to the customers lives.

4. When we look at asset protection from a natural perspective, we realize that in nature, assets are protected not with fences or walls but with internal and external immune systems. So the best way to protect an asset is with systems that self organize and self execute behaviors which function as protective to the asset.

5. The best way to protect an asset is with systems that self organize and self execute behaviors which function as protective to the asset.

6. Business is better able to solve societal problems than charity. Because solutions are sustained anywhere there is a profit motive.

7.

8. The success of a strategy largely depends on it's implementation. You can have a good strategy, you can have a winning game plan, but ultimately you and your team have to implement the strategy and execute and put the game plan into action if your business is going to succeed.

9.

10. With everything in business, the benefits gained should exceed the cost incurred.

11.

12. Mayflower-Plymouth is a company, and it's an ecosystem. We are an Investment Holdings company that holds mostly small and medium sized businesses in our portfolio. And we also provide a variety of resources and business services such as consulting - in the interest of helping businesses to be better.

13.

14.

15. As markets change and the broader economy evolves, new opportunities for businesses to add value emerge. And new possibilities for new kinds of businesses also emerge.

16.

17. In this global economy of rapid change, innovation is not a nice-to-have anymore - it's a necessity. Every employee in the business needs to be innovation capable or innovation adaptive.

18.

19. In business, it's important to be able to make informed decisions.

20.

21. Business done well has the ability to supersede charity.

22.

23. In the permaculture economy, recycling isn't good enough. It's more about upcycling - because as resources cycle through the system, they should continue to add greater value to the system.

24.

25. We can only have a Permaculture Economy when we systematically treat waste as a resource.

26.

27. A dysfunctional society is bad for business. If the society you live in is wasteful or destructive or non-inclusive or inefficient.... It's more difficult to manage a business, and there are less business opportunities available. So every entrepreneur should be concerned about social dynamics and broader society.

28.

29. The key to having a permaculture economy is ensuring that the waste from every one is a resource for another.

30.

31. When every ones waste is a resource for another, an interesting truths emerge - no waste exists in the system as a whole, resources become abundant and easily accessible, businesses become generally more profitable, and wealth becomes more widely distributed. This is a circular economy. This is a permaculture economy.

32.

33. The key to having a permaculture economy is ensuring that the waste from every one is a resource for another.

34.

35. When every ones waste is a resource for another, interesting truths emerge - no waste exists in the system as a whole, resources become abundant and easily accessible, businesses become generally more profitable, and wealth becomes more widely distributed. This is a circular economy. This is a permaculture economy.

36. Bartering has a suite of business applications in today's economy.

37.

38. Every business sets its own pace for growth; the pace of that growth will determine what the business is going to be like in two, three or five years.

39.

40.

41. Business failures are valuable. When you experience failure as an entrepreneur, make a conscious effort to try to understand everything about how you failed and how the business failed. It'll help you succeed.

42.

43.

44. One way to improve your business is to increase its capabilities. The more capable your business is of providing value to it's customers, the more success your business will experience.

45.

46. A business is an ensemble of people. The energies, attitudes and personalities of employees come together and form the energy, attitude and personality of the business.

47.

48.

49. A business is like a living being. It needs to be cared for, loved, stewarded, nurtured, and led.

50.

51.

52. To make good business decisions, you need to be routinely extracting actionable data from the businesses processes. Analyzing the data and organizing it in

alignment with the businesses goals will allow for greater clarity in making decisions.

53.

54.

55. Your products and services should attract customers like pollen attracts honeybees. The value of what your business offers should be a magnet to customers.

56.

57.

58. Social issues impact every business. Whether we're talking about womens health or education or economic equity or climate change or renewable energy... All of these things impact businesses and their ability to profit. And they all present business opportunities also. So there's a lot to consider at the intersection of business and social work. And you can't really care about business without also caring about people's well-being, so every entrepreneur should be a social entrepreneur trying to help other people live better lives in some way.

59.

60.

61. A good business adds value not only to individual people, but also to systems and networks of people. A good business has a multiplicative value effect.

62.

63. From a business perspective, an asset is anything that generates consistent reliable cash flow/revenue. One of the core duties of business management is to nurture business assets to ensure that the business's income continues and grows perpetually. Because ultimately, assets are what make a business a business.

64.

65.

66. At Mayflower-Plymouth, we understand that each business is unique.

67.

68. It's tough being an entrepreneur. You gotta be someone that's tough and knows how to bounce back.

69. It's just as great to be an employee as it is to be an entrepreneur. Great employees add immense value to businesses and therefore to markets and to economies. Being an employee is important.

70.

71.

72. At Mayflower-Plymouth, we pride ourselves on providing holistic solutions. Businesses have problems, cities have problems, society has problems... and we have solutions to those problems. And me being a polymath and the founder of the company means that polymath spirit is embedded in the company's nature. We like to solve all kinds of problems and present all kinds of solutions across various industries.

73.

74. Profit is good.

75. Profit motivates businesses to be:

76. (a) efficient - to do more with less, to consume fewer resources, to reduce and reuse waste.

77. (b) productive - to allow for bigger profit margins.

78. (c) Valuable - income, and therefore profit is only possible when we add value to our customers lives. When the value of our product or service is worth more to them than what it cost us to provide it, we profit.

79.

80. Twrg add
81.

.

82. Money can reach you through many different ways at any moment in time.

    Money doesn't have limits. Be receptive and keep your heart open to the many

    possibilities.

83.

84. I am a value adder. My contributions improve peoples lives and I do it with ease

    and consistency. Therefore, I am a money magnet and money flows into my life

    with ease and consistency.

85.

86. The abundance of money has a significant correlation to freedom. It's good to

    have a lot of money.

87.
88.

89. Small amounts of money can do good things. But big money can do great things.

90.

91. Investing, like spirituality, has a lot to do with energy, frequency and vibration.

    But it takes mastery to figure out how. And then even more mastery to apply the

    knowledge toward desirable results.

92.

93. Every tree in every forest is participating in investment activities..... capital

    allocation, energy flow, resourcefulness, utilization, leverage, information distribution, growth, value creation, and ROI.... Nature is an economy, and

every tree is an investor in that economy.

94.

95. There is a spirituality to money. Things like theft and fraud and dishonesty will

never produce good long-term monetary results. And the ROI for those things is

always a deficit.

96.
97.
98. Gratitude amplifies wealth.

99.

100.   The utilization of productive assets is what investing is about.

101.   Money actually does grow on trees. Money is that abundant. Money is

that available.

102.
103.   La riqueza no es algo seco y estancado. La riqueza es dinero vivo. La

riqueza es dinero vibrante. La riqueza es dinero en movimiento. La riqueza es

dinero que crece continuamente hacia una abundancia cada vez mayor,

produciendo más y más de sí mismo. La riqueza se trata de dinero que fluye con

facilidad, gracia y definición.

104.
105.

106.   Invertir tiene mejores resultados cuando se aprende de la naturaleza.

107.

108.   No necesitas trabajar duro por dinero. Nada en la naturaleza trabaja duro.

En cambio, se trata solo de agregar valor y contribuir bien a la sociedad, ser alegre,

estar abierto a recibir, sentir gratitud y sentirse rico. Haz estas cosas y el dinero

fluye.

109.
110.
111.   El dinero es bueno. Y cuanto más, mejor.

112.
113.
114.   Liquidity equals freedom.

115.
116.   When you have big objectives, you need big money

117.

118.   Si agrega valor y ayuda a otras personas de alguna manera, entonces el

dinero debería fluir en su vida con facilidad.

119.

120.   Money is good. And the more the better.

121.

122.   Saving money is vital to cultivating wealth. You cannot magnetize money if you have a habit of spending all of the money you have. Eventually, money will realize its not safe with you. To magnetize money and accumulate money, you need to be a saver, among other things.

123.

124.   If you have wealth without liquidity, you're still in bondage. If you have capital without currency, you're still in bondage. Liquidity equals freedom.

125.

126.

127.   Money is supposed to flow easily and consistently. We should add value in the world in the way that is most natural to us individually, and money should just naturally flow into our life.

128.

129.   If your adding value and helping other people in some way, then money should be flowing into your life with ease.

130.

131.   Money loves to multiply. Money loves to grow.

132.

133.   If you're adding value and helping other people in some way, then money should be flowing into your life with ease.

134.

135.

136.   Assets are like trees and money is like fruits. The goal is for our trees to produce as much fruit as possible and for us to enjoy in that abundance of fruit.

137.

138.

139.

140.   Having a lot of money is about providing for your family, enjoying the beautiful moments, minimizing stress, and having the liberty to live a heart-centered spirit-centered life. It's good to have a lot of money.

141.

142.

143.   It's good to love money. It's the hatred of money and the lack of money that cause problems.

144.

145.

146.

147.

148.

149.

150.   It's good to always think good thoughts about money. Think loving thoughts about money. Think joyful thoughts about money. Think of money and smile and feel the joy of having so much money. And fill every atom your body with that feeling. This is true wealth.

151.

152.

153.

154.

155.

156.

157.   Money and love make a great couple. Money can do amazing things when it's paired with love. And love can do amazing things when it's paired with money.

158.

159.   Money is beautiful. And the more money I have, the more beautiful it is. And I feel like my money gets more beautiful every single day. And every day, I see more beauty in it as it keeps growing and multiplying and flowing and expanding.

160.

161.

162.   You don't need to work hard for money. Nothing in nature works hard. Instead, it's just about adding value and contributing good to society, being joyful, being open to receive, feeling gratitude, and feeling rich. Do these things and the money flows in.

163.

164.

165.   The concept of 'spending' is problematic. When we are functioning with intention and wisdom, the only thing we really do with money is invest. There are small investments, and big investments. There are good investments and bad investments...The ROI we get for some investments is a product or service - the groceries in exchange for money, or the the car wash in exchange for money. And the ROI we get for other investments may be additional money in the form of interest or dividends, while the ROI in other cases is just a sense of fulfillment after maybe giving to charity or buying a gift for your spouse, or paying for your kids tuition, or creating art.

166.

167.   When we look at it from this perspective, we get rid of the expectation that sending money out is a loss, and we replace it with an expectation that sending money out will always result in an ROI of some kind. Everything is an investment when we act with intention and wisdom.

168.

169.

170.   When money is pooled together, it has a greater impact. A million dollars has more impact than one hundred thousand dollars. One hundred ETH has more impact than ten ETH. The more money, the greater the impact.

171.

172.   There is a correlation between money and happiness. Money is our reward for adding value and helping other people. And we should feel happy about adding value and helping other people and all the rewards we get from that. That should fill us with joy and fulfillment.

173.

174.   Money basically does grow on trees. Money is that abundant. Money is that available.

175.

176.

177.

178.

179.

180.

181.

182.

183.

184.   Wealth is not a stagnant dry thing. Wealth is money alive. Wealth is money vibrant. Wealth is money in motion. Wealth is money continuously growing into greater and greater abundance, producing more and more of itself. Wealth is about money flowing with ease and grace and definiteness.

185.

186.

187.   A major part of wealth is liquidity. Yes, It's important to have valuable assets with big price tags. But it's also important that your assets are doing more than inflating your net worth. Those assets should be providing continuous, substantial and endless streams of money for you.

188.

189.   You should always be able to access the money you need to do the things you need to do and like to do. There is power in liquidity.

190.

191.

192.

193.   Money is better when you have more of it. With money, enough is not enough. You should always have more than enough money - an abundance of money. Look at nature, nature never only makes enough of a good thing. It always makes more than enough. And there's no scarcity or lack. Everything in nature experiences more than enough.

194.

195.

196.   Money is like water, it's everywhere. It's in the ground, it's in the sky, it's in the air... it's everywhere. If you'd like, your wallet or account can be like a rainwater pool where the money is filled up and always flowing. And where you can just put a cup in that pool and drink from it whenever you like and you always have more than enough money because the pool is always full. And there's a prosperous ecosystem where the money clouds are always passing by and pouring more money in there. That's a good relationship with money.

197.

198.

199.   Investing isn't a game - It has a substantive impact on the living of life and the development of civilization. It's not just about stock tickers and opening bells and timing buys and sells to get a quick profit in the gap.... It effects when and where houses are built, the quality of schools, the accessibility of organic food, the price of solar relative to gasoline.... Investments direct the development of civilization.

200.

201.   Investing is a special thing. In terms of functionality, almost anyone invest. But in terms of achieving the results of long-term profit and sustainable growth, only some people have the talent or skill sets for that. It's like baseball for example... anyone can swing a bat at a ball. But only a few guys make it to the big league, and even fewer become world champs. These days there are so many apps and platforms for individual investing, but that doesn't mean everyone is achieving the same results. There are great investors, good investors, and bad investors. A professional investor can achieve exponential growth and profit. A professional investor understands markets and industries and can account for both the traditional and the new.

202.

203.

204.

205.   Money has a spiritual correlation. What we do with money and how we impact the world through our spending, saving and investing.... It has spiritual consequences.

206.

207.   With money comes responsibility. How we spend and invest our money has an impact on ourselves and on so many other people.

208.

209.

210.

211.

212.

213.   There are enough resources in the world for everyone to experience some variable degree of wealth. And from a spiritual perspective, there are no limitations, only abundance.

214.

215.   Money can reach you through many different ways at any moment in time. Money doesn't have limits. Be receptive and keep your heart open to the many possibilities.

216.

217.

218.

219.   The abundance of money has a significant correlation to freedom. It's good to have a lot of money.

220.

221.

222.

223.   Small amounts of money can do good things. But big money can do great things.

224.

225.

226.   Investing, like spirituality, has a lot to do with energy, frequency and vibration. But it takes mastery to figure out how. And then even more mastery to apply the knowledge toward desirable results.

227.

228.

229.

230.

231.   Investing requires vision, patience, research, and strategy.

232.

233.

234.   Our Investments should be consistent with our values

235.

236.

237.   Equity without income is unnatural.

238.

239.

240.   Saving money is vital to cultivating wealth. You cannot magnetize money if you have a habit of spending all of the money you have. Eventually, money will realize its not safe with you. To magnetize money and accumulate money, you need to be a saver, among other things.

241.

242.

243.   Investing at large scales is where the greatest impact happens. When we're investing with billions of dollars or trillions of dollars, it's easier to effect whole systems and implement society-scale results more rapidly and with more efficiency.

244.

245.   When you have big objectives, you need big money. We have big objectives at Mayflower-Plymouth and we have a lot of good things to do in the world that's going to help a lot of people, so we need to be working with big numbers.

246.

247.   It's good for good and spiritual people to have a lot of money. Because when good and spiritual people have a lot of money, we do good and spiritually aligned things with the money.

248.

249.

250.   It's ok to spend money, especially on the necessities and the normal pleasures of life. You should spend money with a knowing that as it flows out, it will flow right back in. Spending is just as natural as income. Income is the breathing in. And breathing out is either investing, spending, or saving. If you don't breathe out, it will cause blockages that turn your money stagnant. We need the inhale and the exhale. It's all about balance.

251.

252.

253.

254.

255.

256.

257.   We all have a responsibility to be efficient stewards of resources.

258.

259.   Investing has the best results when you learn from nature.

260.

261.

262.   Business is supposed to be fun. We're supposed to love what we're doing. Don't let these old folks convince you that business is about spreadsheets and MBA's and metics and all that stuff. That's all good, but ultimately business is just about adding value to other peoples lives and getting them to pay you for it.

263.

264.   In an economy where problems are prevalent, solutions are profitable

commodities. And in an economy where solutions are profitable commodities

and many consultants look to easy profit by productizing things; providing

holistic solutions is a strategic advantage. And that's what we do at Mayflower-

Plymouth. We provide holistic solutions.

265.

266.   Most people don't need to be babied through business processes. Most

often, what they need is a clear understanding of the objective and access to

available resources. From there, they'll leverage their own creative capacity and

skillets to ensure that the objective is accomplished.

267.

268.   Most people don't need to be babied through business processes. Most

often, what they need is a clear understanding of the objective and access to

available resources. From there, they'll leverage their own creative capacity and

skillsets to ensure that the objective is accomplished.

269.

270.   A Permaculture Economy provides the greatest conditions for people and

businesses to thrive.

271.

272.   It's important to address the source of a problem. When you target the source and solve at the source, it prevents that problem from becoming a problem again.

273.

274.   People become more valuable when they gain skills and capabilities that enable them to add value to other peoples lives. A business is a collaboration of people. Businesses also become more valuable when they gain skills and capabilities that enable them to add value to peoples lives.

275.

276.   Every business can benefit from good quality management consulting services. Consultants are able to gather, assemble and utilize data in unique ways. Consultants also have perspectives that are likely to be unique compared to the perspectives you find internal to your business.

277.

278.   With everything we do in business, it's important that we always consider the ecological implications. And if we're really doing things the Permaculture way, then it's not just about factoring in ecological cost, but better yet ensuring

that business processes and outputs actually add value to ecological and natural systems.

279.

280.　　To be successful in business, you need to understand what you're selling and you need to understand the people who are buying. And the more holistic your understanding, the more success the business will experience.

281.

282.　　In business, its very important to do consistent market research. It's very important to understand your customers and potential customers. The more you understand them, the better you'll be able to add value to their lives, and the more they'll pay for that value.

283.

284.

285.　　Leadership requires kindness. If the people in positions of power in the company are cruel and mean to the other employees, it puts the whole company into a fear vibration. And that repels customers. Leaders should be stern, but kind; bold, but gracious.

286.

287.

288.   The Profit function: Individual profits cause collective growth and

prosperity. It is necessary for individual people and businesses to profit in a

Permaculture Economy where justice is maintained and fairly applied. Profits are

earned when efficiency is mastered. With profits, individuals invest in (a) new

and innovative means of production which will allow more profits, or (b) buying

products and services from other individuals who are also seeking profit by

providing value.

289.

290.   Profits also incentivize individuals to be productive participants in society

to begin with. If there will be no profit in an activity, business or industry, then

individuals will decline participation in that activity, business or industry. Since

profits are only possible when buyers are satisfied with the productivity of sellers,

then it is also true that an individuals willingness to participate in an activity,

business or industry is preceded by the buyers satisfaction which allows the seller

to profit. But when buyers are dissatisfied and decline participation, it forces

sellers to decline participation. Inversely, if profits are eradicated through the

force of price-controls by the government, then sellers will decline participation which then causes buyers to decline participation. And when both sellers and

buyers decline participation, then whole industries and economies collapse.

291.

292.   Being valuable is the start. But a good business also has to communicate its

value to its customers and those customers have to also voluntarily be in

agreement with that value. If the customers perceive the value, and determine

that the value they obtain from your businesses products or services is greater

than the value of the dollars, Renminbi or ETH they have in their wallet... then

they will pay for what your business is selling. If not, they won't.

293.

294.   One sure way to increase a businesses profits is to implement a process

improvement program. When a business audits it's internal processes and

extracts waste from those processes, the result is inevitably more time or money

being leftover.

295.

296.   In today's global economy, it's essential that businesses efficiently execute

on or plug into logistics.

297.

298.   When we look at supply chains and distribution in nature, we see that

natural systems include an abundance of nodes in a network. Distribution is

widely spread - enough to include the maximum nodes feasible yet not enough to

add unnecessary time or cost to the path a thing takes from source to destination.

299.

300.   This maximizes efficiency, and minimizes the risk of congestion and

bottle-necks.

301.

302.   It's best to magnetize your business to specific kinds of customers;

customers that are aligned with the businesses goals, purpose, and values.

303.

304.

305.   The first priority of the business is to add value to the customers lives, in

exchange for payment.

306.

307.

308.   We all have a responsibility to be efficient stewards of resources. That's

also what good investing is about - being an efficient steward of resources.

309.

310.	Efficiency is a major key to business success. It's good when a business can do more with less. Not out of scarcity but out of efficiency. When a business does more with less, the result is more revenues produced from less investment... More revenues produced with less expenses... more customers attracted with less marketing activity.... More savings with less trade-off... Businesses that do more with less are rewarded with greater profits and greater capital.

311.

312.

313.	Margins matter in business. If a business has $1,000,000 dollars in revenues but $1.5 million in expenses, the business is heading for self destruction due to a liquidity problem. Meanwhile, if another business only has $100,000 in revenues and $50,000 in expenses, it's doing better than the first business even though it has less revenues. And a business with $60,000 in revenues but only $2,000 in expenses technically has a greater margin than both of the other businesses. Revenues are very important, but the key is to both maximize revenues and minimize expenses so that you have the widest profit margin possible.

314.

315.   Our Investments should be consistent with our values.

316.

317.   It's simple. If we value health, we shouldn't have our money plugged into businesses and systems that promote disease. If we value spirituality, we shouldn't have our money plugged into businesses and systems that promote a perversion of the spirit.

318.

319.   Business ideas are sensitive to market conditions, culture, technological development and other things. What maybe was a bad business idea ten years ago may be a great business idea today. Give it a try. Mayflower Plymouth.

320.

321.   If you run a business, it's essential that you love whatever the business is selling. What you have with the business is similar to what you have with any other relationship - it will experience more success when love and passion is poured in.

322.

323.   If a businesses customers can clearly describe its value proposition, then it has succeeded in its marketing plan.

324.

325.   Our Investments should be consistent with our values.

326.

327.   If we value the environment, we should have our money invested in businesses and systems that improve the condition of the environment and add value to nature. If we value health, we should have our money invested in businesses and systems that help people to live healthier lives in some way.

328.

329.

330.   It's good to celebrate the value your business adds. Every employee in the business should celebrate the value the business adds. What you celebrate, you give life to.

331.

332.

333.   Whether your business sells Reiki healings or Jeans, Custom Pottery or YouTube Meditations, Computer Software or Construction materials....

Business fundamentals remain business fundamentals... Create value,

communicate value, sell value.

334.

335.

336.   Efficient supply chain management is essential for individual businesses,

specific markets, and for the economy as a whole - especially when we're talking

about Permaculture Economics. A global economy where products and services

are moved from source to destination with maximum efficiency.... That's a win

for everyone.

337.

338.

339.   In order to have a healthy economy, we need both entrepreneurs and

employees. We need business of every size and we need people to accept the

many jobs offered by those businesses. So it's okay to celebrate entrepreneurship,

but let's also celebrate the good things about being an employee.

340.

341.   If your business doesn't have money set aside in a business savings

account, then your business is extremely vulnerable to crisis. Your business has

gotta put money aside as a safety precaution.

342.

343.   In business, it's really important to keep operating costs low. You don't

want your business to be a spendthrift business because spendthrift businesses

eventually eat through all their earnings.

344.

345.   If your business can substantially cut costs and pass along those cost

savings to customers... Then your business will likely experience an increase in

demand for it's products or services.

346.

347.   3D Printing has a major role to play in the circular economy.

348.

349.

350.

351.   In business partnerships, it's important to do your due diligence and

eliminate as much risk from the deal as possible.

352.

353.

354.   There's a lot to consider at the intersection of business and social work. It's about earning a lot of money while adding a lot of value to peoples lives and making the world a better place.

355.

356.

357.   One of the greatest joys of leading a business is providing jobs to other people.

358.

359.   Timing is important in business and in life. Time is infinite, and ultimately there is only the present. But time is also kind of a living moving thing and it moves in rhythms. Every business should try to move in harmony with these rhythms.

360.

361.

362.

363.

364.   Location matters when it comes to business. Whether its physically or virtually or both, its important to have a presence where your clientele are present.

365.

366.

367.   Profit is good.

368.   Profit compells people to be:

369.   (a) efficient - to do more with less, to consume fewer resources, to reduce and reuse waste.

370.   (b) productive - to allow for bigger profit margins.

371.   (c) Valuable - income, and therefore profit is only possible when we add value to our customers lives. When the value of our product or service is worth more to them than what it cost us to provide it, we profit.

372.

373.   And there's no scarcity of possible profits. Every business should be profiting. When every business is profiting, that's a lot of increased value going around.

374.

375.

376.

377.   Good cities cultivate welcoming business environments.

378.

379.

380.   With managing a business, you need to Invest in good software and or good data mining systems. Run your numbers routinely. Take a look at your revenues - when is the money typically coming in, from where, can you identify any patterns in your revenues? Then take a look at your expenses - analyze the numbers and identify patterns. Why? Because Identifying patterns and extracting actionable items from your revenue and expense data will result in the clarity you need to make good business decisions.

381.

382.   The goal is to have customers who appreciate the value your business is selling; and customers who are willing and able to pay for that value.

383.

384.

385.

386.   Companies can learn a lot from biological systems. The human immune system for example is adaptive, redundant, diverse, modular, data-driven and network collaborative. A company that desires not just short term profit but also long term resilience should apply these features of the human immune system to it's business models and company structure.

387.

388.

389.   A good Board Of Directors team is one where ideas are flowing fluidly - and where each idea is met with an initial welcome, an intellectual challenge, an expression of gratitude, a rigorous scrutiny and a readiness for action.

390.

391.   Technology has always been and will always be a disruptive force in business. And it will always be the case that businesses that are rigid and stagnant and unimaginative will die. And businesses that are adaptive and resilient and imaginative will continue on living.

392.

393.   Crises often come with hidden opportunities. When we approach crises with this awareness, we can look for the opportunities and then leverage them.

394.

395.

396.

397.   Additive manufacturing has a major role to play in the circular economy.

398.

399.   Business is supposed to be fun. We're supposed to love what we're doing.

Don't let these old folks convince you that business is about spreadsheets and

MBA's and metrics and all that stuff. That's all good, but ultimately business is

just about adding value to other peoples lives and getting them to pay you for it.

400.

401.   At Mayflower-Plymouth, we like to invest holistically. We consider

profitability, we consider peoples wellbeing, we consider the environment and so

much more.

402.

403.   Nature is the greatest school of business.

404.

405.   Every business should own, at minimum, a general liability insurance

policy. The business needs to protect itself and mitigate against risk.

406.

407.　　As long as businesses have problems that need solutions, consultants will be valuable.

408.

409.　　Individual profits cause collective growth and prosperity. It is necessary for individual people, businesses, and companies to profit, in a Permaculture Economy where justice is maintained and fairly applied. Profits are earned when efficiency is mastered. With profits, individuals invest in (a) new and innovative means of production which will allow more profits, or (b) they use profits to buy products or services from other individuals who are also seeking profit by providing value. Profits also incentivize individuals to be productive to begin with. If there will be no profit in an activity, business or industry, then individuals will decline participation. Since profits are only possible when buyers are satisfied with the productivity of sellers, then it is also true that an individual's willingness to participate in an activity, business or industry is preceded by the buyers satisfaction which allows them to profit. So, when buyers decline participation it forces sellers to decline participation. Inversely, if profits are removed through force of price controls by the government, then sellers will decline participation which then causes buyers to decline participation.

410.

411.   Business management requires its own skill set separate from being skilled at whatever service or product the business provides.

412.

413.

414.   A business is not just a legal entity - it's a group of people engaged in the voluntary exchange of products, services, agreements and currencies. Buyers and sellers determine whether a business is a business. Not it's legal entity status given by the state. I think legal status is good, but it's not what truly establishes a business.

415.

416.

417.   In today's constantly evolving economy, business models cannot be static. The business model of each business must be consistently changing and evolving in order to stay relevant and to succeed.

418.

419.

420. In todays complex economy, managing a business or company can be nuanced and complicated, but the fundamentals remain the same. Create value, communicate value, sell value. There may be a thousand other things to consider and specific tasks to do, but the fundamentals remain and they remain vital. Create value, communicate value, sell value.

421.

422.

423. In terms of business resilience, it's important to have the ability to repurpose inputs and redirect outputs. It's important to have a good amount of flexibility designed into the businesses operating systems. When a business can answer the if this then that question over and over again with different fill in the blanks, it's got resilience.

424.

425.

426. A major determinant of a businesses success is the productivity of its employees.

427.

428.

429.   If you're adding value and helping other people in some way, then money should be flowing into your life with ease.

430.

431.   Assets are like trees and money is like fruits. The goal is for our trees to produce as much fruit as possible and for us to enjoy in that abundance of fruit.

432.

433.

434.

435.   Businesses are at all times and in different ways accountable to employees, suppliers, customers and community.

436.

437.

438.   Ultimately, Investing is about holistic ROI. It's not about just owning stocks or crypto or flipping for quick income. When we talk about holistic ROI, we are looking at our long term profit, short term profit, income security, cash flow, social impact, environmental impact, spiritual impact, stability of the permaculture economy, and more.

439.

440.

441.

442.

443.   A good investment is like a good fruit tree. From its conception, it grows exponentially larger consistently and reliably. It's required input in a small percentage of its output. It regularly gives back to the broader ecosystem, helping multiple other lives to prosper. And it produces an abundance of fruit for the enjoyment of its owner.

444.

445.

446.

447.   Business is a lot like gardening. And you have to tend to your business the way you tend to plants in your garden.

448.

449.   When money is pooled together, it has a greater impact. A million dollars has more impact than one hundred thousand dollars. One hundred ETH has more impact than ten ETH. The more money, the greater the impact.

450.

451.　The way to stay in business is to keep solving problems and providing solutions to a considerable amount of people at the highest price point possible. And society is always evolving, so we should always keep looking out for new problems to solve and new kinds of solutions to provide and new ways to add value.

452.

453.　Starting a business is risky. But with every risk, there are substantial rewards. Successful entrepreneurs learn to keep their minds focused on the rewards.

454.

455.　Profits are a standard, not a priority. The business should price its products and services maximally above its expenses. But the priority and main focus should always be adding value to the customers lives.

456.

457.　At Mayflower-Plymouth, we're here to help your business figure this out, and to provide holistic solutions.

458.

459.

460.   A good investment is a productive investment.

461.

462.   As companies age they tend to become more reliant on extracting value

from their past successes and less desirous of innovating. It's every CEO's job to

ensure the company rejects this tendency and instead chooses to embrace both

the capital of past success and the capital of present innovation.

463.

464.

465.   Algorithms are great tools for improving business results, but its people

and their leadership that ultimately determine business success.

466.

467.   In business, profitability is a non-negotiable.

468.

469.

470.   Managing a business does not require any genius. The main qualification

is the ability to identify and deliver value to a group of people consistently and efficiently at the highest price point acceptable to them. Everything else can be hired out.

471.

472.   The customers should be happy, but the business should not accept mediocre profits just to make the customers happy. The relationship between business and customer should be reciprocal.

473.

474.

475.   Insurance is important in business. It just makes sense that we share risk for low probability high impact events.

476.

477.   When we ask ourselves what is an economy; I think the best place to find the answer to that question is in a forest. Go and sit in a forest and observe with all of your sensory faculties, and meditate there. And while you're observing and meditating, ask yourself questions about everything.

478.

479.   And you'll find out exactly what an economy is. And you'll also find out exactly what business is. And all of the economic and business concepts like

capital allocation and liquidity and service and profit and growth... It'll all start to make more sense as you sit there meditating in that forest.

480.

481.   Businesses need to save and invest just like individual people do. Every business should be accumulating capital and cultivating growth.

482.

483.

484.   In business, supply chains risks are not only correlated to the competition or to collaborators or to customers. Supply chain risk is also correlated to all of the companies and industries using the same imputs as your business.

485.

486.   People buy from businesses for many reasons. Among those reasons include: favorable price, favorable accessibility, demonstrated shared values, label identification, and more. The more reasons you can give people to buy from your business, the better sales numbers your business will experience.

487.

488.

489.

490.

491.   A major part of wealth is liquidity. Yes, It's important to have valuable

assets with big price tags. But it's also important that your assets are doing more

than inflating your net worth. Those assets should be providing continuous,

substantial and endless streams of money for you.

492.

493.   You should always be able to access the money you need to do the things

you need to do and like to do. There is power in liquidity.

494.

495.   Money is better when you have more of it. With money, enough is not

enough. You should always have more than enough money - an abundance of

money. Look at nature, nature never only makes enough of a good thing. It

always makes more than enough. And there's no scarcity or lack. Everything in

nature experiences more than enough.

496.

497.   Money loves efficiency.

498.

499.   In business, what's required for short term profit and what's required for

long term resilience are very often at a juxtaposition.

500.

501.

502.   Things nature is good at include - organizing matter in a way that is multi

functional, mass customization, network adaptation to circumstance, responsive

evolution, growth as a mechanism for construction, decentralization, data

management and asset management. Regardless of what kind of business we are

talking about, there's something vital to learn from nature.

503.

504.   Investing, like spirituality, has a lot to do with the flow of energy.

505.

506.   When we are talking about cash flow - once again, nature is a great teacher.

Cash is simply the base resource with which most activities predicate. In nature,

cash is symbolized by water. Rarely is anything in nature ever lacking water. Even

in the deserts, the life forms that live and grow there have figured out 'cash flow'

or 'water flow'.... They've figured out how to manage the flow of water relative

to the tasks and objectives which require its use. If a cactus in the desert can figure out how to manage the flow of water relative to the tasks and objectives which require its use... then we can figure out how to manage the flow of cash relative to the tasks and objectives which require its use. If nature can invest wisely, so can we.

507.

508.   Investing is a special thing. In terms of functionality, almost anyone invest. But in terms of achieving the results of long-term profit and sustainable growth, only some people have the talent or skill sets for that. It's like baseball for example... anyone can swing a bat at a ball. But only a few guys make it to the big league, and even fewer become world champs. These days there are so many apps and platforms for individual investing, but that doesn't mean everyone is achieving the same results. There are great investors, good investors, and bad investors. A professional investor can achieve exponential growth and profit. A professional investor understands markets and industries and can account for both the traditional and the new.

509.

510.   Investing is a special thing. In terms of functionality, almost anyone can invest. But in terms of achieving the results of long-term profit and sustainable

growth, only some people have the talent or skill sets for that. It's like baseball for example... anyone can swing a bat at a ball. But only a few people make it to the big league, and even fewer become world champs. These days there are so many apps and platforms for individual investing, but that doesn't mean everyone is achieving good results or ROI. There are great investors, good investors, and bad investors. A professional investor can achieve exponential growth and profit. A professional investor understands markets and industries and can account for both the traditional and the new.

511.

512.   Investing has the best results when you learn from nature. Planet Earth has been alive for much longer than you or I and and it this thing figured out.

513.

514.   Money has a spiritual correlation. What we do with money and how we impact the world through our spending, saving and investing.... It has spiritual consequences.

515.

516.	Every tree in the forest knows about creating value, and about reciprocity

and about stewardship. And every tree in the forest knows about profit and

about investing and about ROI. This is why I study and learn from nature.

517.

518.	With money comes responsibility. How we spend and invest our money

has an impact on ourselves and on so many other people.

519.

520.	When you invest in something, you establish an energetic connection with

it. So be careful what you invest in, and invest wisely.

521.

522.

523.	Our society today celebrates entrepreneurship way too much. It's great to

be an entrepreneur. But it's also great to be an employee. In order to have a

healthy economy, we need both entrepreneurs and employees. We need business

of every size and we need people to accept the many jobs offered by those

businesses.

524.

525.   At the end of the day, the business needs to be profitable if it's going to keep providing the products or services that the customers love. If you're a customer and you love what you're buying from a business, then you should want that business to be profitable so that you can keep on buying that stuff from them.

526.

527.   As a business owner, you should be looking at data as a key resource to help you make more informed decisions that ultimately allow you to grow revenues and maximize profits.

528.

529.   When you're leading a business, you have to pay attention to what's going on in the economy as a whole. When economic paradigms shift, you better shift your approach to business accordingly.

530.

531.   Growing a business is a lot like growing a fruit tree. Ideally, a fruit tree will yield a lot of fruit from a little bit of soil rain and sun. And ideally, your business will yield a lot of profit from a little bit of capital.

532.

533.   Business leaders a hundred years ago thought about business with a very mechanical way of thinking. But today and going forward, business leaders need to think about business with a biological and energetic way of thinking; thinking of business in terms of living systems.

534.

535.

536.   Businesses profit by solving social problems. Therefore, it's business - not charity or government - that should be employed to solve many of the big societal problems of today. Whether it's the climate crises, or gender equity, or pollution or whatever... Business can solve those problems.

537.

538.

539.

540.   It's good to include playful and imaginative activities in business management. Managers of every business should be actively utilizing their imagination and directing that toward the advancement of the business. And incorporating playful activities into managerial routines is a good way to do that.

541.

542.

543.

544.　　In nature, there is no such thing as waste. Every output is upcycled into new inputs of equal or greater value. This creates a cycle of productive utility, continuous growth and continuous expansion.

545.

546.

547.　　The real cost of something is its value in alternative uses. This truth always presents itself in prices. There is no benefit that may be gained without cost to the same individual who gained the benefit. There is no benefit that may be presented without cost to the same individual who present the benefit.

548.

549.

550.

551.

552.　　Every business has to prioritize protecting its assets.

553.

554.   In business, profitability is a non-negotiable. If a business is not profitable, it's worthless.

555.

556.

557.   An idea is not a business. It doesn't matter how wonderful your idea sounds. What matters is the revenue model and how the business is going to earn money consistently, sustainably and abundantly.

558.

559.   Popularity is not profit. Ultimately, what makes a business is it's profitability. Popularity can convert to profit but it does not equal profit. Likes and follows are nice, but business is all about sales.

560.

561.

562.   Every business experiences loss, but loss should be temporary. The overwhelming financial story of a business should be profit.

563.

564.   Leadership requires kindness. If the people in positions of power in the company are cruel and mean to the other employees, it puts the whole company

into a fear vibration. And that repels customers. Leaders should be stern, but kind; bold, but gracious.

565.

566.

567.   How a business presents itself is very indicative of that businesses sense of self and about how much value and respect it's owners and employees attribute to it. If the owners and employees don't respect the business, neither will the customers and potential customers.

568.

569.

570.   Being a skilled professional at something does not automatically equate to being skilled at leading a business in that same profession. Someone could be a phenomenal hair stylist, but that doesn't mean that they would be a great manager of a Salon. Business management requires its own skill set separate from being skilled at whatever service or product the business provides.

571.

572.

573. Maintaining good accounting records is vital to the successful management of a business. It's really good to be able to assess business-specific financial data to inform decisions. So every business should invest in good accounting software like Intuit, Quicken, or Freshbooks... Or any of the many apps out there.

574.

575.

576.

577. If a business isn't efficiently utilizing resources, then it's a bad investment. A wasteful business is an unprofitable business. That may or may not show on their P&L for the current year, but you better believe it shows somewhere.

578.

579. Humans as a species will need to embed the concept of symbiosis into our global society such that in all of our activities - we are voluntarily benefitting from and providing benefit to a multitude of other life forms. And businesses should be leading the way with this.

580.

581.   Productivity should emerge from a natural flow, not from force. If you are working in alignment with your purpose and skill sets, you will have a certain work-flow that naturally results in productivity. And that productivity can be further improved with intentionality. In this way, your investment of time and energy achieves the maximum ROI.

582.

583.   NFT's are transforming the way commerce is transacted, contracts are enforced, investments are held, and value is transferred.

584.

585.   A business that doesn't respect human life, animal life and the ecosystem of our planet earth... that's a business we don't want in our portfolio. If the business does more harm than good, facilitates more death than life, and causes more destruction than creation... then we view them as a bad investment.

586.

587.

588.

589.   The greatest investment you can make is in yourself. Invest in the resources and opportunities you need for you to be your best self. When you are

your best self, and I am my best self, and everyone else is their best self.... Then

everything else will be subsequently better. That's some great ROI right there.

590.

591.   Value earned is according to value provided.

592.

593.   If you're a customer and you love what you're buying from a business,

then you should want that business to be profitable so that you can keep on

buying that stuff from them.

594.

595.   If we want better global supply chains, there are lots of other things that

have to be made better first. We need to be better with equitably including small

businesses into global logistics. We need to be better with upcycling, and

feedback loops. We need to be better with implementing Blockchain technology.

We need to be better with material ecology and designing products for longevity.

And so much more.

596.

597.

598.　　Online and in-store experiences should work together to drive sales for the business.

599.

600.　　Global supply chains have many constituents and responsible parties. Everyone in the supply chain has a responsibility to act in a way that promotes effeciency in the supply chain.

601.

602.　　You have to be a optimistic person to succeed as an entrepreneur. Fear and pessimism are dangerous to entrepreneurs.

603.

604.　　Business is not a popularity contest. Views and likes and follows are all important. But ultimately your business is measured by what's on the P&L and whats on the Balance Sheet. Ultimately, businesses are measured in money.

605.

606.　　There are so many ways to add value to peoples lives. But what's also important is monetization. The key is to find that balance where your business is efficiently monetizing the value that it's adding.

607.

608.

609.   Business is not a popularity contest, it's a sales campaign. Popularity is

only good if it converts to sales. Influence is only good if it converts to profit.

610.

611.

612.

613.   How your business makes your customers feel has a direct correlation to

how much money they are willing to spend with your business and the

promptness with which they spend money with your business. You should make

your customers feel welcome, make them feel appreciated, make them feel

respected. And show customers that your business is valuable by ensuring that

you and every employee treats the business with care and respect.

614.

615.

616.   In business and in all of life, a major part of effective crisis management is

acknowledging the existence of the bad things that are happening. Once you

have that acceptance, you can begin to strategize step by step how to manage the crisis and emerge from the crisis into a more favorable reality. But if you pretend like the bad things aren't happening, they magnify the crisis.

617.

618.   As a business owner you should never mix business income with personal income and never mix business expenses with personal expenses. Your business is a separate entity with a life of its own. Your job is to lead and manage that separate entity, not to entangle with it. Entangling with your business will result in chaos. But keeping business and personal separate will facilitate efficiency and reduce stress.

619.

620.   A business is in alignment if it's employees feel a sense of fulfillment from working for the business and its customers feel a sense of fulfillment from buying from the business. In this case, fulfillment is in both the exhale and the inhale of the businesses activity. And this cycle of fulfillment will lead to sales and profits.

621.

622.   There are lots of ways to measure a company's success. You can look at earnings reports and get really specific with the numbers. You can look at social capital and the influence the company has on people. You can look at the balance

sheet and the value of its assets. You can look at its legal framework, it's brand, it's staff.

623.

624.   The key to valuing a company is to look at the company holistically.

625.

626.   For any business to endure in today's ever changing global economy, there has to be a willingness and an ability for that business to consistently renew itself and redefine itself and revitalize itself.

627.

628.   In business, when it comes to implementing change, there's a lot of redefining that often needs to happen... that might include redefining budgets, redefining resources, redefining business processes, and redefining value.

629.

630.   There's power in intuitive organic growth. Sometimes businesses thrive by just taking it one step at a time as opposed to having some grand strategy. Strategy is really important in business, but so is intuition.

631.

632.   When new things emerge in our world, its best to put some time into

researching them and trying to gain an understanding. With that understanding,

you're then able to think about and plan for the new business applications for

those things and the new ways in which your business may profit from them.

633.

634.   One of the major prompts for businesses implementing change is the

evolution of technology. As new technologies emerge or new use cases emerge

for existing technologies; markets are forced to reorganize and therefore

businesses are prompted to reorganize in response to that.

635.

636.   When a business is experiencing dysfunction, it often times has a lot to do

with internal processes and internal systems. And when we put in place new

internal processes and new internal systems based on clear objectives and a clear

value-add strategy, the business transitions from dysfunction to effectiveness.

637.

638.

639.   Organizational restructuring is something that should take place within a

company fairly regularly. With our modern day economy being as dynamic as it is, and with change being as prevalent as it is, companies need to be adaptive and

flexible - and that requires regular restructuring.

640.

641.   Transitioning a business from current state to future state requires clear

strategy, adaptability, synergy among all involved and a dedication to execution -

among other things.

642.

643.

644.   When a business utilizes resources wisely, it becomes better able to widen

the margins between revenues and expenses.

645.

646.   Every Spring, nature teaches a class on business entrepreneurship. ....We

see how capital is re-allocated, currencies are re-directed, growth is re-emphasized,

and numerous life forms promote their value with re-vitalized marketing

programs that implement flowers or seeds or aromas or habitability or

pollination in an effort demonstrate a unique value proposition in a busy

economy.

647.

648.   Smart entrepreneurs enroll in this class every Spring and take good notes. Whether you're an entrepreneur of a small business or an entrepreneur of a line of business within a large company... learn from nature.

649.

650.   Every Spring, nature teaches a class on business entrepreneurship. ....We see how capital is re-allocated, currencies are re-directed, growth is re-emphasized, and numerous life forms promote their value with re-vitalized marketing programs that implement flowers or seeds or aromas or habitability or pollination in an effort demonstrate a unique value proposition in a busy economy.

651.

652.   In nature, waste does not exist. There is only production and consumption; there is only creation and utilization. Everything that's produced is efficiently consumed. Everything that's created is efficiently utilized. And this cyclicality results in growth and in profit. The same should be true of each business, and the same should be true of an economy.

653.

654.   Sus productos y servicios deben atraer clientes como el polen atrae a las abejas. El valor de lo que ofrece su negocio debe ser un imán para los clientes.

655.

656.   Transitioning a company from present state to future state is not just about the company at large, but also about every single employee and customer and partner also transitioning from present state to future state. We have to consider the macro and the micro if the transition is going to be successful.

657.

658.

659.   When we're talking about businesses adapting to change, it's not just about the processes and systems but also about people and their ability to practice new relationships, methods and behaviors.

660.

661.   Organizations seek to implement change because they acknowledge that the present version of the business is insufficient and that to ensure business continuity the business must manifest a new version of itself.

662.

663.   As more companies comitt to Corporate Social Responsibility, the result

is the emergence of a Permaculture Economy and a more prosperous world.

664.

665.   In this new age where data is so abundant, our task as a civilization now is

effective beneficial utilization. The challenge now is doing good things with that

data - things that make our lives and the lives of future generations of people

more fulfilling and more joyful and more prosperous.

666.

667.

668.   A circular economy is a step in the right direction towards a permaculture

economy.

669.

670.   Businesses are better positioned in cities that prioritize sustainability.

671.

672.   For example, business leaders look at the architectural environment -

whether or not the buildings in the city designed for efficiency and resiliency.

Business leaders look at energy - whether or not solar and other renewable energy

sources are designed into the city's systems. And business leaders look at a variety of other factors regarding sustainability when they're deciding where to establish or relocate a business. So cities that prioritize sustainable development are positioning themselves to be hubs of business success.

673.

674.   Some people like to hate on big companies because they're big. I like to learn from big companies because they're big. In business, size is a measurement of success. It's certainly not the only measurement. But it is an important measurement.

675.

676.   There's a difference between managing a business and leading a business. They require two different skill sets.

677.

678.   Change Management provides value in part by enabling people to adopt the change and operate in the future state of the company.

679.

680.   When we're talking about implementing change in business, it's good have a holistic view and to consider all of the dynamics, including: What is the scope of the change? Who is being impacted (customers, employees, others)? How are

people being impacted, and in what way? Are there different perspectives regarding the experience of the change? What exactly is being changed (systems, processes, jobs)? What is the expected timeline for the change?

681.

682.   In business, technology is a wave that you just have to surf. Businesses either surf the wave, or they drown in it.

683.

684.   When changes are being implemented in a company, it's usually the case that the extent to which people are invested in the current status quo is the extent to which they will resist the proposed changes. So the key is to get everyone divested from the old status quo and invested in a new status quo.

685.

686.   El negocio se trata de crear valor para un grupo específico de personas.

687.

688.

689.   Si quieres tener un negocio rentable, necesitas tener un negocio eficiente.

690.

691.

692.   Cuando una empresa agiliza sus procesos, inevitablemente experimenta

otros beneficios que pueden incluir una mayor satisfacción de los empleados,

más ganancias, una mejor contabilidad y más.

693.

694.   La economía siempre está cambiando. Por lo tanto, su negocio siempre

debe estar cambiando. Administrar un negocio incluye adaptarse al cambio,

evolucionar con el cambio y, a veces, ser pionero en esos cambios y evoluciones.

695.

696.   La mejor manera de proteger un activo es con sistemas que se organicen y

ejecuten comportamientos que funcionan como protección para el activo.

697.

698.   Una empresa es como un ser vivo. Necesita ser cuidado, amado,

administrado, nutrido y dirigido

699.

700.   Los negocios bien hechos tienen la capacidad de reemplazar la caridad.

701.

702.   Our Investments should be consistent with our values.

703.

704.   Everything is energy. If you are invested in a company that is actively involved in destroying forests, or slaughtering animals, or polluting oceans or promoting disease... then so you are passively involved in those same activities.

705.

706.

707.   There are a lot of business opportunities emerging in relation to human space exploration. As we explore our solar system and eventually our galaxy, there will be plenty of new business ventures and lots of value to be added and lots of money to be made with that.

708.

709.   As data and science become more accessible and more the production of software and AI, human creativity is becoming a more valuable commodity.

710.

711.   You can't approach business the same way you approach an algebra equation or something. When you're considering the viability of a business, you have to also consider the psychology of human beings, the logistics of peoples emotions, cultural factors, sociopolitical factors, peoples habits, and more.

There's a lot to consider when you're thinking about what people are going to

pay for and how much they'll pay and why they'll pay and what they really value.

712.

713.   To succeed in business, it's important to be good with numbers.

714.

715.

716.

717.   There isn't much room for ego in leading a business. The business will

experience the greatest success when the leaders and employees of the business

focus less on self and more on pleasing customers.

718.

719.

720.

721.

722.

723.   If your business asset has expenses that are directly correlated to revenues

and they take up a big percentage of revenues, and you determine that it is not

possible or practical to reduce the expenses or increase the associated revenues for that asset - you have two options: If in totality the assets revenues are greater than its expenses, keep the asset and do not get rid of it. Small profit margins are better than no profit margins and this asset is adding value to your business's portfolio. If the assets expenses are greater than its revenues, then it is actually not an asset and any decisions made about it should be made with this realization in mind.

724.

725.   You don't need degrees or diplomas to be successful in business - you just need an understanding of what people value and how to sell it to them. Now if you have degrees and diplomas in addition to that, then even better.

726.

727.

728.   A lot of people are talking about the circular economy. But the ultimate goal is to have a permaculture economy.

729.

730.

731.

732.

733.   When your company is contemplating change, it's important to take

inventory of employees perception. Does everyone in the company understand

the need for making the changes being contemplated? And is everyone in the

company committed to the changes? These are important considerations.

734.

735.   Employees aren't inanimate objects that can just be moved around like

bricks. They're people with emotions and goals and comittments and more. They

should be treated like stakeholders, because they are.

736.

737.   Only when people agree on goals can they agree on methods. Only when

people agree on the destination can they agree on the route. Only when people

agree on the past and present facts can they cooperate to co-create new and

mutually desirable facts.

738.

739.   Business is about making peoples lives better.

740.

741.

742.

743.   Liquidity is essential in business. So many businesses fail because of a failure to retain liquidity. But the principle is simple - to get things done, businesses need access to cash and capital. And without that access to cash and capital the business will fail because it won't be able to find it's operations.

744.

745.   Business is about making the world a better place.

746.

747.   To succeed in business, it's important to have an understanding of markets.

748.

749.

750.

751.   Many modern businesses have become proficient at mining data. In fact the mining of data is becoming almost routine. But as we advance further into the 21rst century and the 22nd century, the utilization of data begins to take priority. So it's not just about collecting all this data, but also about getting really creative with generating new ways to utilize that data in the quest to add value.

752.

753. Good companies have a good impact on all of its stakeholders. Everyone that the company interacts with should experience a value-add of some kind. And every environment in which the company operates should experience a value-add of some kind. And if done right, this will also drive up profits for the company.

754.

755. A reality whereby all individuals live, work and play together in a system of harmony and continual reciprocity, and in the spirit of love and unanimity – is possible. And we living today are the ones to make it happen.

756.

757. Businesses everywhere can learn a lot from nature.

758.

759. Biomimicry is known for its design applications. But biomimicry also has an abundance of business applications. When businesses learn from nature and apply what they learn; the results include greater efficiency and more profit, among other things.

760.

761.

762.   Putting coalitions in place that consist of various stakeholders is often

times crucial to a successful change management implementation.

763.

764.   The global economy and all of its markets are constantly changing. In

order to survive and thrive as an individual in business these days, you've got to

be always updating your mental models. You've got to be always updating the

software of your mind and spirit so that you remain capable of seeing the new

ways value is being measured and exchanged; and so that you remain capable to

plugging in to and profiting from the new ways that value is being exchanged.

765.

766.   Thriving through change requires clear strategy. But ironically, it also

requires the willingness to toss all of your existing plans out the window if the

business is presented with new data or new circumstances that delegitimize the

clear strategy.

767.

768.   When a company is implementing vital changes, it's going to include some

discomfort. Anytime we forego the comfort of the known even in search of something better, it's still a little bit uncomfortable as we transition from one state of being to another state of being.

769.

770.   Effective scaling requires clear strategy. Nature has provided us with a portfolio of growth applications to learn from and our job as business leaders is to be strategic with that.

771.

772.   To thrive in business, it's good to have a clear understanding of the laws that affect business.

773.

774.

775.   The human dimension of organizational change is vital. Because ultimately, a company is a collaboration of people.

776.

777.

778.

779.

780.

781.   Your products and services should attract customers like pollen attracts honeybees. The value of what your business offers should be a magnet to customers.

782.

783.

784.   When your business prioritizes the wellbeing of all of its stakeholders, then all of those stakeholders gain respect for the business and your business can utilize that respect as a sort of currency and a means to accomplish business objectives.

785.

786.   Marketing is not about looking good or getting likes or gaining more followers. Marketing is about getting your product to market or getting your service to market. If your marketing efforts aren't converting to sales, then your marketing efforts are failing.

787.

788.   The value of a company has very little to do with it's stock price.

789.

790.

791.   If your company doesn't continue to innovate, your company isn't going

to be around much longer.

792.

793.   Effective communication is essential in business!

794.

795.   As a new entrepreneur, you're probably gonna have to hustle hard to get

things going at first. And you gotta be committed to that hustle until it's not

necessary anymore.

796.

797.   Businesses are born, businesses live, and businesses die. And that's okay.

798.

799.   Businesses are like people in many ways - we expect them to live long,

prosperous and productive lives but we also know they won't live forever.

800.

801.   Every company should have a good internal mentoring system in place.

802.

803.   If you want your business to be resilient, you gotta improve cash flow and

widen margins.

804.

805.   If you wanna make money in business, you gotta train yourself to see the world from a business perspective.

806.

807.   Don't be that employee that complains all the time! Instead, be that employee that sees opportunities within the business and weeks to collaborate with colleagues and management to make the business better.

808.

809.   Don't be that employee that complains all the time!

810.

811.   Even as an entrepreneur, you need to see yourself as an employee of your business.

812.

813.

814.   Jobs make the world go around.

815.

816.   There's no age mimimum to entrepreneurship. Kids can be entrepreneurs, kids can be executives. Ultimately succeeding in business is about the skill and

capacity to add value. If you have that skill and capacity to add value as a kid,

then you'll succeed in business.

817.

818.

819.

820.   Good leaders are balanced people. They're both decisive and thoughtful.

They're both curt and kind. They're both focused and considerate of broader

realities.

821.

822.   If you treat your employees like trash, they will treat your customers like

trash. If you treat your employees beautifully, they will treat your customers

beautifully. A good business treats it's employees beautifully.

823.

824.   If marketing is taking up 1/3 of your revenues or more, something is

wrong. Yes you've gotta get the word out about your products and services,

especially if you're in a saturated market. But your products and services should

attract customers like pollen attracts honeybees. The value of what your business offers should be a magnet to customers. You shouldn't be chasing after customers begging them to do business with you.

825.

826.

827.   One way to assess the viability of a business idea is to consider it's ability to be monetized. If something can't be monetized, it ain't a business. And if there's no path to profitability, then it has no worth.

828.

829.   Likes, views and follows are nice, but business is all about sales. If your likes, views and follows don't convert to sales and money in the business bank account - then from a business perspective those likes views and follows are worthless.

830.

831.   There are a lot of external factors that impact the success of a business. Local city infrastructure, local public health and the local school system are each examples of this.

832.

833.   Marketing is not about looking good or getting likes or gaining more

followers. Marketing is about getting your product to market or getting your

service to market. If your marketing efforts aren't converting to sales, then you're

marketing efforts are failing.

834.

835.

836.   As an employee, you should care about the profitability of your employer.

If the company you work for is succeeding in the marketplace, that means more

job security for you.

837.

838.   If your business is behind on it's bills, you know your business has a cash

flow problem. And cash flow problems will destroy a business quickly.

839.

840.   If we want a circular economy; a permaculture economy - we need to

design decay into products and processes as opposed to disposability.

Manufacturers should design materials and products to programmatically

biodegrade back into an economic ecosystem. This will allow for more efficient

upcycling and the cultivation of various business opportunities in the process.

841.

842.   If we can teach young people about the essentials of business while they're young, they'll be better business people when they're older.

843.

844.

845.

846.   As a new entrepreneur, you're probably gonna have to hustle hard to get things going at first. But as the business grows and becomes more established, that unrefined hustle should be replaced by automated profit-producing processes and systems. Hustle is good as a temporary mode of operating, but it's unsustainable long term and unprofitable long term.

847.

848.

849.   As a new entrepreneur, you're probably gonna have to hustle hard to get things going at first. And you gotta be comitted to that hustle until it's not necessary anymore.

850.

851. You have to include inflation in your annual revenue and expense forecasts. You have to treat inflation as an annual fee your business pays into the economy. If inflation is 2% for example, that means the economy is charging your business a 2% annual fee and so you gotta make sure your income and total assets grow at minimum 2% annually just to keep up.

852.

853. Sometimes a business has to lose money in its infancy. But that's only okay if there's a path to profitability and a clear vision of a profitable business model. A loss is only acceptable if it's a present investment into future profit.

854.

855. In business, all expense projections and all revenue projections must account for inflation.

856.

857. Pricing power is important in business. You want your business to have the flexibility to raise prices as needed, especially with regard to inflation.

858.

859. If you have to constantly reinvest the business profits back into the business just to keep the business going, then your business has a major cash flow

problem. If your business has thin margins like that, it is incapable of resilience. If you want your business to be resilient, you gotta improve cash flow and widen margins.

860.

861.   Business credit should be utilized to facilitate income growth and expense reduction. If you view business credit as liquidity you're going to get into trouble because on the receiving side, credit is a liability not an asset - It has to be paid back out of future income. So think about that. Your business can only pay back a loan plus interest if future income is greater than present income and future expenses are less than present expenses. To put it bluntly, credit must facilitate profit.

862.

863.

864.   Imagination is a valuable commodity in business, especially these days. Your business won't survive if it's people lack imagination.

865.

866.   It's a good feeling when your business has paid all of it's bills.

867.

868.

869.   Authenticity is important in business, and in every part of life. Be true to yourself, and make sure the business is being true to itself.

870.

871.   Businesses need to have goals, just like people need to have goals.

872.

873.

874.

875.   Transparency is a good quality to have in business. Honesty, integrity and transparency will gain you the right customers and the right investors. And dishonesty always results in long term losses.

876.

877.

878.   When employees see each other as teammates and encourage each other to do a better job, everyone in the company shares in the rewards.

879.

880.   You get teamwork in the workplace by giving teamwork in the workplace. It's not only about your personal career success or your colleagues' personal

career success, but it's also about the success of the company - which is good for everyone employed at the company.

881.

882.

883.   As managers, we should hire people whose values align with the values of the company, and then trust them to do their job well. If you have to micromanage an employee, one of you isn't a fit for the company.

884.

885.   One of the great themes of nature is abundance. One of the great themes of every city should also be abundance. In every city, there should be an abundance of opportunities, an abundance of food, an abundance of available homes, an abundance of biodiversity, an abundance of spaces to play.

886.

887.   Investing requires vision, patience, research, and strategy.

888.

889.

890.   If you're an entrepreneur and you've started a business that you're growing from the ground up, just know that its okay to get a job somewhere else

while you build up the business. For probably most entrepreneurs, that's just part of the journey. There's no shame in that.

891.   —

892.

893.   As the economy evolves and new technologies emerge that change the way value is exchanged, the kinds of things that we call assets also evolve and change. Assets in 2022 encompass a much broader scope of things than assets in 1922. And assets in 2050 will include new things that maybe don't even exist today or old things that have new roles. The definition of an assets doesn't change, but the kinds of things that are assets changes as society changes.

894.

895.   Profit seems to be a natural phenomena. In nature, everything seems to have an innate inclination to in some ways produce more value than it consumes, while also in other ways gaining more value than it spends. Everything in nature seems to profit the whole with the value it creates and seeks to profit itself with the value it consumes. This is business.

896.

897.   The role of charity is to fill in the gap where business has not yet

discovered or executed a profitable path at maximum distribution.

898.

899.   Climate change is something that matters to businesses. This is an issue

that has the ability to impact the potential of businesses, the profitability of

businesses and the opportunities present in the economy.

900.

901.

902.   There is no shame in failure. Everybody who has ever lived has

experienced failure throughout their life, whether they will be honest about that

or not.

903.

904.   When you're humble, people tend to be more forgiving with your failures.

I've learned to just be humble and keep my ego tamed. This gives me the freedom

to live transparently without fearing what people will think about my failures.

905.

906.   Everybody has problems. There's no need to be ashamed of the problems

you're experiencing. There's no need to hide them or pretend like your life is perfect. It's actually better to expose your problems because only when problems are exposed can solutions find them. Only when problems are exposed can they be solved. I learned this lesson the hard way.

907.

908.   We are all called to lead in some ways and we are all called to follow in some ways. Both leadership and followership are good.

909.

910.

911.   Complication is sometimes necessary in business, but all else being equal, simplicity is always better. Try not to get your business into situations that are difficult to extricate it from.

912.

913.

914.   In business, it's very important to protect your businesses income! Because a business with no income is not really a business at all. As long as the business has income - even if margins are slim, you can find a way to cut expenses, improve cash flow and improve it's profitability. Tight cash flow can be better leveraged than no cash flow. But if you make choices that jeopardize or forefeit

the income, because you're frustrated with slim margins, then you forfeit that opportunity. Work with those slim margins while you work on widening them.

915.

916.   Hustle is to business success what fossil fuels are to civilization. It's extremely important in the beginning, but eventually you gotta upgrade to something more efficient and something more sustainable.

917.

918.   It's good to exercise the imagination and fantasize about unique new business ideas and innovations. But ultimately, every idea has to comform to practical application. Sometimes ideas can be willed into existence, and sometimes it's better to comform and try to fit into the status quo. But either way, to be successful in business you have to succeed at practical application.

919.

920.   Nature is quite unwelcoming to unprofitable things. It seems to be a non-negotiable in nature that every thing in nature must produce more value than it consumes.

921.

922.   It's not about in store versus online, or physical versus virtual... business in

this century is often but not always about omni-channel distribution and getting

leads and sales through a variety of platforms that may include all of the above or

unique combinations.

923.

924.

925.   When your employees enjoy holistic health, your business is better able to

add value and serve it's customers.

926.

927.

928.   It's not about Bitcoin or Ethereum or NFT's... These things have merely

shown us what's possible. But the real value is in Cryptography, Blockchain

Technology, Cryptocurrency and Smart Contracts - these are the things with the

real business implications.

929.

930.   A good manager is always looking to cultivate talent in people, and a good

manager is always looking to find employees doing something right so they can give compliments and encourage the team to keep doing the good things they're

doing.

931.

932.   A good manager is more eager to compliment peoples strengths than they

are to criticize their weaknesses.

933.

934.   A good leader is more interested in giving compliments than critiques.

935.

936.   Leadership is about helping other people to be better.

937.

938.

939.

940.

941.

942.

943.

944.   Sometimes you gotta just give the customers what they want.

945.

946.	business has no minimum age. If you're 13 years old and you have a great

business idea, you don't have to wait until you reach a certain age or until you

graduate high school or anything like that. You can be in business right now and

be successful at it. Growth takes time, but it's never too early to get started.

947.

948.	Having the cash is only part of the solution. Once your business has the

cash, the real task now is to invest it wisely and in a way that'll result in growth

and greater profit.

949.

950.

951.	Dont alienate your existing customers in search of new customers. A good

approach is to continue to do what makes your existing customers happy, while

doing additional things that attract new customers without alienating your

existing customers. And in some cases, it's more advantageous to do better by

your existing customers instead of looking for new customers.

952.

953.

954.	It's a good idea to either have a cost accountant on payroll, hire a cost accountant to audit your business twice a year, or invest in good cost accounting software.

955.

956.

957.	Your business would not have any income if it wasn't for it's customers. So it's very important to always and openly express gratitude for the customers.

958.

959.

960.	As an entrepreneur, you should definitely stay aware of what's going on in the economy. But don't let economists tell you how to do business.

961.

962.

963.	Debt is just as dangerous in business as it is in personal finance. Entrepreneurs need to be careful not to cripple the businesses they lead with debt. Because one thing debt does well is cripple it's host.

964.

965. Sometimes debt is a useful tool that can help the business achieve it's strategic goals. But be careful - because one thing debt does well is cripple it's host.

966. Everything is always changing in business, except the essentials. Markets change, platforms change, customers change, owners change, trends change.... But the essentials remain constant.

967.

968. Each business is like a poinciana tree - it produces a blossom of some kind that is a gift to the world.

969.

970. It's important to always keep the business' assets growing. Inflation will make sure that expenses grow, so each business needs to make sure that it's money is growing.

971.

972. When a company relies on future sales to pay off existing debts, it's in a risky situation. That's a gamble that often results in bankruptcy.

973.

974.   When a company experiences new kinds of competition, it needs to

urgently become a new kind of competition.

975.

976.   Honesty is very important in business. It's important to customers, it's

important to investors and it's important to markets.

977.

978.   Sometimes the economy is unpredictable. Sometimes markets and

industries are unpredictable. Sometimes unpredictable things happen that could

impact the company. That's why your company needs to have a healthy amount

of liquidity; accessible cash. And that's why the company needs to be nimble and

able to adapt. A nimble and adaptable company with healthy cash reserves is

better positioned to thrive even through unpredictable circumstances.

979.

980.   A nimble and adaptable company with healthy cash reserves is better

positioned to thrive even through unpredictable circumstances.

981.

982.   Airline frequent flyer mile programs are a great case study for

cryptocurrency. Trends change, markets change, people change. And every now and then there's some new fancy thing we're all talking about. But if you look deeper you realize the core essence of that new fancy thing is actually pretty old. Trends change, markets change, people change - but the essentials of business don't change.

983.

984.   Trends change, markets change, people change - but the essentials of business don't change.

985.

986.   It's good to be transparent in business. As much as possible, the business should be transparent about it's products and services. And it should be transparent about it's income, expenses and debts. Transparency fosters trust. And trust is very valuable in business.

987.

988.   Failure is amazingly normal in business. In business, failure is common and typical. So the key is to build resilience and fortitude into the business so that it can overcome failures and optimize successes.

989.

990.   Each business should try to learn from the little failures so they can avoid

the big failures. And at the same time, try to celebrate the little successes and

maximize the scope of its big successes.

991.

992.   It's hard to keep operating a business with little cash, little sales, high debt

and decreasing asset values.

993.   Traders have no concern with the intrinsic value of a company. They only

care about stock price.

994.

995.   Companies can bounce back just like people can bounce back.

996.

997.   One of the biggest killers of business is an unwillingness to adapt.

998.

999.   Timing is critical to a successful product launch.

1000.

1001.   A system that utilizes bartering and smart liquidity is superior to a debt

based system.

1002.   Putting work in for your business is good. Your business needs you to put

that work in. But don't exhaust yourself because if you drain yourself to the

point of exhaustion then you become a liability to your business.

1003.

1004.   Business models are never inherently good or bad. Business model success

is relative to the industry, to what's going on in the economy, to the specific

business, to the year and more.

1005.   The brand of the company is important. Ask yourself - when people hear

the name of the company, what are the first five things that come to mind? The

aggregate of the first five things that come to mind for everyone will illustrate the

authority of the company brand.

1006.

1007.   Leverage amplifies risk. So that risk better come with nearly guaranteed

profits.

1008.   Your company should not gamble with leverage. Companies shouldn't

gamble on borrowed money. If the company is going to borrow and leverage

other peoples money, it should be going toward something profitable, stable and

safe.

1009.

1010.   If a company gambles on leverage, it'll probably go bankrupt on leverage.

1011.   With everything you do in business, you have to factor in the tax

implications.

1012.   If your business is making you go broke, it's doing the opposite of what it

should be doing.

1013.

1014.   A lot of people confuse investing with arbitrage. Someone who buys

stocks with the express hope that the stock price will rise so they can sell it and

pocket the difference between what they bought it for and what they sold it for -

that person is not an investing. What they're doing is arbitrage.

1015.

1016.   Arbitrage is not investing.

1017.

1018.   Sometimes companies prioritize market share over profitability. That may

be a good short term strategy, but it's unsustainable and there's a strict time limit

on that whether company leadership will admit it or not.

1019.

1020.   If your business is getting into debt, you gotta ask yourself what is the cost of servicing that debt. Do a simple cost benefit analysis. If the cost of servicing the debt

1021.   A company can accept lower margins when it has less debt. Debt forces prices up and because of the risk it adds to the company, it also forces continuous wider margins.

1022.   When industries lack competition, businesses get belligerent. Competition helps keep businesses humble.

1023.

1024.   Expanding into rapidly growing markets is way easier than trying to grow into stagnant and highly competitive markets.

1025.

1026.

1027.

1028.

1029.

1030.   You can learn a lot about business by watching sports. Some of the

strategies you see being executed in a game can actually be translated into

business terms and executed to achieve business success.

1031.

1032.   In business, you gotta provide value. Technologies evolve and sometimes

new technologies enter the mix. New apps, new platforms, new patterns of

consumption, new ways to produce.... The ways value is produced and

consumed is endlessly changing. But the necessity for businesses to produce value

and the desire for the buyer to consume value; that never changes.

1033.

1034.   Equity without income is unnatural.

1035.

1036.

1037.

1038.

1039.   Banking is transforming. What a bank will be in 2030 is going to be

significantly different from what a bank has been for the last few hundred years.

1040.   Data is one of the most valuable resources of a bank.

1041.

1042.　The kind of data and the data-analytical perspective privy to banks is quite unique to banks.

1043.

1044.　At their core, banks sell the utility of resources and the stewardship of resources.

1045.　It's great to have and accumulate cash, but much of the time in business, from an operational perspective, it's more practical to forego cash and instead just barter for the thing that the cash is buying.

1046.

1047.　When we pair modern tech like Blockchain technology, cryptography and data analytics with the ancient practice of bartering, a lot of business opportunities emerge.

1048.　Independently, new technologies can be pretty impactful to businesses. But the whole world in which businesses operate changes with the convergence of many new technologies. So we need to always be mindful of how technologies are converging and how that convergence may pressure us to adapt how we think about business and how we do business.

1049.

1050.   Because of the subjectivity of needs and the subjectivity of value, bartering can be just as good as cash in business transactions.

1051.

1052.   When we apply the principles of permaculture to business operations - we end up with more profitable businesses, more resilient businesses, and businesses that holistically add value to all stakeholders.

1053.

1054.   When businesses are having liquidity problems, bartering can be a solution.

1055.   By bartering with certain things, it opens up space that allows the business to use cash more strategically and on the most profitable things.

1056.

1057.   When people have responsibility without authority, they're unable to direct progress.

1058.   As society evolves, the possibility for new business models emerge.

1059.

1060.   The decisions you make in the boardroom eventually show themselves in company performance.

1061.

1062.   Businesses, like people, should have multiple sources of income.

1063.   In business, having a good reputathttps://g.co/kgs/it5pgBion is imperative. Because trust is a prerequisite of commercial relations. Whether it has to do with investing, shopping at a store, or getting into a collaborative deal... We go with what we trust and we go with who we trust. We invest in what we trust, we shop where we trust, we partner with who we trust.

1064.

1065.   Within the industries where businesses typically Ft Right with tight margins, bartering provides even more of an operational advantage w and the stewardship is it busy with a talent and a readiness we w we. And by incorporating bartering into those industries, wider margins can maybe become more typical.

1066.

1067.   In regard to the health of planet Earth, business should be a value adder.

The sum of global business activity should actually add value to natural

ecosystems.

1068.   In order for a business to scale, it has to improve efficiencies. Efficiency is

a prerequisite for sustainable scaling.

1069.

1070.   Business and politics are antithetical. If you wanna succeed in one, stay

out of the other.

1071.   Teamwork is a critical component of success in business.

1072.

1073.   It's good when employees enjoy working with each other and contribute

to each other's productivity. That's an indicator of synergy within a company.

1074.

1075.   Companies with healthy cultures enjoy a healthy existence.

1076.

1077.   Good management has a lot to do with incentives and decentives. It's

about making sure the company has systems in place that incentivize desired

behaviors and decentivize undesirable behavior.

1078.

1079.   Company culture has a lot to do with company success.

1080.

1081.   A lot of business is collaborative, and a lot of business is competitive. And it's important to know when to focus on which.

1082.

1083.   In business, qualitative measurements and quantitative measurements are equally important.

1084.

1085.   Entrepreneurship requires passion! It's so challenging being an entrepreneur and sometimes a little bit lonely too, so you really need to love what you're doing.

1086.

1087.   Regulatory compliance is critical to managing risk.

1088.

1089.   You gotta be smart with AdSpend. Ultimately it's about conversion to sales. And that AdSpend needs to have a healthy ROI based on that conversion to sales.

1090.   It's really important for ads to be personalized. It's important for

potential customers to see reminders of themselves in your advertising.

1091.

1092.   If you can enable the customers and potential customers to make

informed purchasing decisions, you increase the likelihood each person will

purchase your products and services.

1093.

1094.   The more you know about your customers, the better you can offer them

things they value at a maximum price point.

1095.

1096.   Mayflower-Plymouth is a business ecosystem.

1097.

1098.   When you're running a public company, you're held accountable to a

multitude of stakeholders all of whom require explanation for your performance.

1099.

1100.   Every business has its own story and its own personality.

1101.

1102.   Net Income is more important than gross revenues.

1103.

1104.　Use the data from the clients you already have to help you find new clients just like them. Eventually you'll be tuned into a whole market segment.

1105.　Whereas gross revenue speaks more to a businesses pricing power and scale, net income speaks more to it's efficiency and operations.

1106.

1107.　Businesses want to plug into the Mayflower-Plymouth ecosystem because in this ecosystem, good businesses become better.

1108.

1109.　Measure Omni channel impact accross all e-commerce and brick and mortar stores

1110.　You wanna make your marketing as dynamic as your customers.

1111.

1112.　In business, sometimes you just have to let the results speak for themselves.

1113.　At Mayflower-Plymouth, we're in the business of business.

1114.

1115.   We all live and work in a dynamic and ever-changing economy. The businesses that are able to adapt, pivot and restructure as needed are the businesses that are most positioned to thrive through the changes.

1116.

1117.   You can't effectively run a company without having clarity on it's key performance indicators.

1118.   In nature, waste does not exist. There is only production and consumption; there is only creation and utilization. Everything that's produced is efficiently consumed. Everything that's created is efficiently utilized. And this cyclicality results in growth and in profit. The same should be true of each business, and the same should be true of an economy.

1119.   In nature, waste does not exist. There is only production and consumption; there is only creation and utilization. We need to model nature in how we manage our businesses.

1120.   Permaculture is an even higher standard than ESG. Whereas ESG is a compartmentalized approach to evaluating businesses, permaculture is a holistic approach to evaluating businesses.

1121.

1122.   At Mayflower-Plymouth, we're into making good businesses better.

1123.

1124.   When we come together, we can increase our bargaining power.

1125.

1126.   Resume's are incapable of holistically communicating a candidates value.

1127.

1128.   Every job is an important job. If it wasn't important. Businesses dont

create jobs and choose to pay people wages or salaries unless it is vital to the

operations of the business.

1129.

1130.   A brand is not a business. But a brand is a business enabler. A good brand

magnetizes customers, incentivizes sales and encourages loyalty.

1131.   If the global supply chains are too fragmented, they're more vulnerable to

shock. And that presents a threat to businesses everywhere. And when businesses

everywhere suffer, people everywhere suffer.

1132.

1133.   When your employees are happy at work, they do a better job. And when

they do a better job, customers feel it. And when customers feel that happiness coming from a companies employees, it's like they just wanna spend their money there.

1134.

1135.   Employment is a social thing and not just a transactional thing. Good salaries and wages are good. Perks and benefits are good. But also, having managers and leaders in place who are kind and genuine and caring towards employees - having that type of atmosphere at the company - that contributes a lot to employee happiness and employee productivity.

1136.

1137.   The best ones to solve the climate change problem are businesses all around the world. If each business adapts permaculture principles, we would see massive improvements in climate and natural ecosystem conditions.

1138.   If you want your employees to feel happy at work and to have a sense of loyalty to the company,

1139.   Employees need to feel trusted and respected at work. Everyone at the company should feel that trust and that respect.

1140.

1141.   Honest accounting is a really important part of corporate responsibility.

Let's just be honest and transparent with the numbers. No inflating, no

exaggerating, no reconfiguring... Just pure numbers that tell the honest truth

about the companies financial status.

1142.

1143.   The idea is that businesses that are plugged into the Mayflower-Plymouth

ecosystem should have competitive and comparative advantages over non

members in their respective markets.

1144.

1145.   To make progress on climate, we need systemic change, not incremental

change.

1146.   Any type of business we're talking about – in any industry, any market,

anywhere in the world – it boils down to this same fundamental truth, the same

fundamental essence and that is: creating value for others and adding some kind

of benefit to the lives of other people.

1147.

1148.   Business is really a altruistic kind of process.

1149.

1150.   Of course we receive payment from customers and clients for the value we

provide. But we receive that payment in exchange for making their lives better in

some way.

1151.   The main thing is identifying a group of people or groups of people in

society or in a marketplace - then identifying what problems they may have, what

needs they may have and what desires they may have - and then formulating

products or services or both that can solve those problems, meet those needs and

fulfill those desires.

1152.

1153.   When we think about business from this perspective: creating value for

other peoples lives, solving problems for other people, meeting other peoples

needs, fulfilling other peoples desires and receiving payment for those good

things that we're doing - the ideas and the creativity flow more fluidly. Because

there's

1154.

1155.   There's always problems to be solved. As long as the economy is changing

and evolving - which it has always been doing, is doing, and will always do - as long as that process is happening - the process of continual change, there will be

problems that need solving. And therefore, there will be business opportunities.

1156.

1157.   As long as people are alive and breathing, they will have needs that need

fulfilling. And therefore there will always be business opportunities there.

1158.

1159.   As long as humans have human nature, they will have desires. Mkay. And

the fulfillment of those desires means that there will always be those business

opportunities.

1160.   We want to maintain alignment with a way of thinking about business

from a value adding perspective.

1161.   If you're trying to make money in business but you're not adding value for

other people, you're not gonna make money.

1162.

1163.   If you wanna make money in business - great! The way to do that is to add

value to other peoples lives. Solve their problems, meet their needs and fulfill

their desires. If you do those things, you're in business and people will pay you

money to do those things.

1164.   The core essence of business is creating value or adding value for other people. And those other people we call customers or clients.

1165.

1166.   Businesses, like people, have purpose.

1167.

1168.   A business's purpose should be aligned with adding a certain kind of value: meeting certain kinds of needs, solving certain kinds of problems, and fulfilling certain kinds of desires. And when the business is doing those things, the business itself feels a sense of fulfillment.

1169.

1170.   When you have a business and people in a business that are feeling fulfilled because they're adding value to other peoples lives and they're making money because of that- you've got a win win win win win win situation - everybody's winning. Customers and clients are winning because their lives are improving with the services or products that the business provides them. Business managers owners and employees are winning because they're receiving compensation and a sense of fulfillment for the value they add. And because these two groups of people are winning, society as a whole is winning.

1171.   If customers and clients are happy - living more fulfilled lives, living more

joyful lives, more abundant lives... If business owners, managers and employees

are happy - living more fulfilled lives, more abundant lives, more peaceful lives...

Of course that's going to ripple out into society. That joy, that fulfillment, that

abundance - it's going to ripple outwards and effect many other groups of

people.

1172.

1173.   In business, value adding and the compensation received for adding value

- it has a ripple effect. And it's a very altruistic ripple effect.

1174.

1175.   We'll have better communities, better cities, better states, better nations,

and a better world - simply because businesses are creating and adding value for

other groups of people. That's the power, the depth and the magnitude of the

core essence of business.

1176.

1177.

1178.

1179.

1180.   Don't show weakness any empathy. Don't show doubt any empathy.

Make a decision, and act on that decision.

1181.

1182.   At some point, we reach maximum efficiency and hard work is not

necessary. But until then, you better work like crazy.

1183.

1184.   You have to be willing to accomplish your goal by any moral means

necessary.

1185.

1186.   Self discipline is extremely valuable as an entrepreneur. If you lose

everything, but you still have self discipline left, you'll get back everything you

lost and multiples more.

1187.   Don't let circumstances determine your comittment level. Worthy

comittments are prioritized regardless of circumstance.

1188.

1189.   Charlotte North Carolina is one of the greatest cities on earth in regard to

business and entrepreneurship.

1190.

1191.   When you're thinking about where is the best place to start a business, there's a lot to consider - It's about culture, it's about physical infrastructure, it's about how educated the people are, it's about the housing, it's about the natural ecosystem, it's about the regulatory and legal frameworks, it's about the local transportation system and the efficiency of all the other systems that are there.

1192.

1193.   Be okay with being doubted at the beginning of your entrepreneurial journey. Unfortunately, it's common for people to doubt entrepreneurs in the early stages of the journey. But if you keep working and building and manifesting and cultivating growth, your success will eventually vindicate you.

1194.

1195.   At the beginning on your entrepreneurial journey, many of your successes are hidden in the darkness, and people don't see them. But if you stay consistent and persistent, eventually your successes are made public in the light.

1196.

1197.   We are each responsible for results. When every employee in the company has this mindset of personal responsibility, the whole company is better for it.

1198.

1199.   If you lead a small business, it's important to understand how to deal with

each credit bureau. TransUnion is the superior credit bureau of the three. They

provide quality and comprehensive reports and they have professional and

intelligent staff. On the other hand, Equifax is mediocre at best. And Experian is

so horrible they're practically garbage.

1200.

1201.   Greenwashing is a problem. That's why the practice of just sticking a label

like ESG on a company isn't good enough. We need to have a the systemic

approach. And we have to approach it from the groung up with systems design,

not from the top down with labels.

1202.

1203.   Mayflower-Plymouth has started a Permaculture Index as an alternative to

the Dow Jones, the S&P, the Nasdaq and the Nikkei. The purpose of the

Permaculture Index is

1204.   Regenerative .

1205.

1206.   Some environmentalists argue that infinite growth is not possible on a

finite planet. And it illustrates how even they are conditioned by traditional capitalist and socialist philosophical frameworks. Exploitation and

overconsumption are only possible in traditional capitalist and socialist systems.

Contrary to both capitalism and socialism, a Permaculture system is regenerative

by design. In a permaculture system, continued growth, upcycling and yield are

designed into the system such that there's a positive feedback loop which

continues endlessly. A forest is a good example of this. Forests everywhere have

found a way to have continued growth, upcycling and yield over billions of years.

That's permaculture.

1207.

1208.   It's important to empower localized problem Solving in the way mycelium

networks do

1209.   Adaptive collective action is superior to bureaucracy.

1210.

1211.   There are a multitude of benefits that arise when we use stigmergic

coordination for collective benefit in our business ecosystems.

1212.

1213.   Cryptographic tokens can be used as tools of stigmergy to incentivize

good behavior and decentivize bad behavior in the context of business systems.

1214.

1215.

1216.   Tokens and Cryptocurrencies can be used to help coordinate human behavior at scale.

1217.   Game theory has a lot of practical applications in terms of business networks.

1218.

1219.   When we bring businesses together in symbiotic relationships, we end up with a system that is much greater than the sum of its parts.

1220.

1221.   The same way biodiversity is important to biological ecosystems, business diversity is important to economic ecosystems. It's good to have an abundance of various kinds of businesses. This cultivates resilience in the system.

1222.

1223.   There are major economic opportunities in human waste. Instead of flushing it down the toilet as waste, we should find ways to upcycle it at scale into various systems as a resource that adds value and facilitates cyclicality.

1224.

1225.   As we design permaculture systems, there's a lot to learn from mycorrhizae

and fungi.

1226.   The way fungi and mycorrhizae direct nutrients in biological ecosystems is

a case study for how we can direct resources within human economic systems.

And in doing this, we cultivate a multitude of business opportunities.

1227.

1228.   In a way, plants are the business ventures of fungi. To fungi, plants are

long term investments that provide enormous yield.

1229.

1230.   The real potential of Web3 is in allowing businesses and people to

collectively function more similarly to biological ecosystems.

1231.

1232.   When we get business networks to function similarly to neural networks

and mycelium networks, we'll have a better world.

1233.

1234.   A business that exploits the suffering of living beings is not worthy of

profit.

1235.   Mayflower-Plymouth is to businesses what mycorrhizae is to trees.

1236.

1237.   In a purely capitalist system, people are taught to approach business as a

very competitive thing. But in a permaculture economy, it's more about

collaboration, cooperation and coordination.

1238.

1239.   Bartering is a common practice in natural ecosystems.

1240.

1241.   Technology is important. We should utilize technology as a tool to help

cultivate a permaculture economy. As we ensure that various technologies

converge within the context of permaculture design and permaculture ethics, we

make the world a better place.

1242.

1243.   Intellectual Property Rights can be used at scale as a method of achieving

collective goals.

1244.

1245.   True cost accounting based on permaculture design principles considers.

1246.   When we find synergy among various technologies like Quantum

computing

1247.

1248.

1249.

1250.

1251.

1252.

1253.

1254.   When you put your business' roots into the Mayflower network, you're

plugging into a network based on permaculture design principles. Our ecosystem

is unique and our ecosystem offers unique value.

1255.

1256.

1257.   The value we provide exists at the culmination of various technologies and

studies including Blockchain, cryptography, quantum computing, artificial

intelligence, stigmergy, additive manufacturing, big data,

1258.

1259.   Mayflower is a member only business service provider.

1260.

1261.   By combining supply chains, we maximize space utilized per vehicle, we streamline routes, we remove waste from the system, we do more in less time, and we provide superior value to the businesses in the network.

1262.

1263.

1264.   Slime mold can teach us how to establish better supply chain networks.

1265.   Biomimicry is critical in regard to using design as a way to solve problems in business. Biological ecosystems have invented solution after solution to all kinds of problems. The key is to learn to see nature through nature's eyes, and to speak nature's language and then to establish a continuous translation between biological ecosystems and business ecosystems.

1266.

1267.   Everything in business that involves the movement of resources can be improved by learning from fungi.

1268.

1269.   At Mayflower-Plymouth, we are trying to mimic the intelligence of fungi and mycelium to add value in service to businesses.

1270.

1271.   Our ports wouldn't have backlogs if our supply chains, distribution

systems and transportation systems mimicked fungal networks.

1272.

1273.   There's relevant data, and there's irrelevant data. In business it's important

to only utilize relevant data.

1274.

1275.   We aren't so much concerned with global or national data metrics. Our

focus is on our internal data metrics and the feedback we get from businesses

within our network.

1276.

1277.   In terms of business ecosystems, complexity is natural and good -

complication is not. The capacity for efficiency is the difference between

complexity and complication. Something can be complex and efficient. But a

thing cannot be complicated and efficient.

1278.

1279.   We are using data as a way to identify large scale patterns and narratives

and then use that insight exclusively in service of the businesses in our network.

1280.   We serve businesses that are typically not plugged into such data networks. And if they are, they're usually data networks whose business models are based on capturing internal data and selling it externally.

1281.

1282.   When your company is buying from my company and my company is buying from your company, there's flow. And if a bunch of our companies are doing that, then that flow can be leveraged toward liquidity.

1283.

1284.   When you're buying from me and I'm buying from you and we're all buying from each other, there's flow within the ecosystem. And businesses in our ecosystem can tap into a portion of that flow to facilitate liquidity for their specific business.

1285.

1286.   In closed loop systems, flow facilitates flow. Liquidity amplifies liquidity.

1287.   In closed loop systems, flow facilitates flow and liquidity facilitates liquidity. Rainforests dont run out of water because of the cycles and relationships between the elements in the rainforest ecosystem. Business ecosystems can facilitate liquidity in the same way.

1288.	Can we train an AI to exist in service to the efficiency of a business ecosystem? I'd like to explore that possibility.

1289.

1290.	Everything we need to know about upcycling, we can learn from fungi.

1291.	When we start learning from and working with fungi, there will be no such thing as trash anymore. And there are so many business opportunities in that.

1292.

1293.	Managing waste is a really dumb goal. Only an inefficient system would aim to manage waste. A better goal is making waste non-existent by designing the system itself through it's participants to continually upcycle resources.

1294.

1295.	Fungi are decentralized intelligence networks. They send information multi-directionally, they constantly evolve and adapt based on feedback from their environment, they invent new molecules to collaborate... And they form a decentralized consensus on how to utilize resources, when to reproduce and what strategies to employ. This is how businesses and business ecosystems should be.

1296.

1297.   Fungi protect the ecosystem they inhabit through complex symbiotic relationships. We can design a system whereby businesses protect the business ecosystem through complex symbiohtic relationships.

1298.

1299.   Fungi broker resources between species via mycelium networks and in doing so they cultivate health and resilience for the entire ecosystem. In the same way, each business should cultivate health and resilience for the entire business ecosystem.

1300.

1301.   When supply can't keep up with demand, the result is bidding wars. And in bidding wars, there are always winners and there are always losers. There are no mutually beneficial outcomes. So from an economic perspective, this is extremely wasteful.

1302.   When supply can't keep up with demand or demand can't keep up with supply, it's indicative of waste in the form of misallocated capital.

1303.

1304.   Most times it's not a single big mistake but a series of small mistakes that

crush a business.

1305.

1306.   When you're a startup entrepreneur, every decision you make is critical to

the survival of the business. There's no unimportant decision. Every decision

matters.

1307.   It's unwise to make plans based on hope. In business, prudence is greater

than hope. And strategy is greater than wishing. Be ambitious, make your

affirmations, and have faith - but also be prudent and practical.

1308.

1309.   Economies transform at the convergence of technologies. It's never a

single technology that changes everything because technologies are always

interdependent with other technologies. And sometimes when a few amazing

technologies converge, it's enough to completely transform society.

1310.

1311.   If there are gaps of unproductive capital in the system, everybody loses.

And when capital productivity is maximized, everybody wins.

1312.   In a permaculture economy, all capital is productive capital and all resources are efficiently utilized.

1313.

1314.   Every problem in society is caused by or correlated to the inefficient utilization of capital. How do we solve the problems in supply chains? More efficient utilization of capital. How to we solve climate change problems? More efficient utilization of capital. How do we end poverty? The more efficient utilization of capital. How do we improve our education system? The more efficient utilization of capital. How do we transition from fossil fuels to sustainable energy sources? The efficient utilization of capital. Simply by striving to efficiently utilize all capital everywhere, we will by default solve a multitude of problems.

1315.

1316.   Simply by striving to efficiently utilize all capital everywhere, we will by default solve a multitude of problems

1317.

1318.   When the human species figures out how to efficiently utilize capital, many of the problems that have haunted us for a long time will cease to exist.

1319.

1320.   The accumulation of capital is a good thing. When we look at nature, we

see the accumulation of capital everywhere. But accumulated capital usually

works in harmony with the productivity of capital. Plots of soil work in harmony

with the forest; and each exists in service to the other.

1321.

1322.   What we are doing at Mayflower-Plymouth is facilitating the efficient

utilization of capital.

1323.

1324.   Nature is really good at capital productivity and capital allocation.

1325.

1326.   Nature is really good at capital productivity and capital allocation. Every

leaf on every tree is positioned to maximize photosynthesis. Every root on every

tree is positioned to maximize nutrient sequestration. And all of the leaves and all

of the roots live in service to each other.

1327.

1328.   Blockchain technology has a lot of potential in service of the efficient

utilization of capital.

1329.

1330.

1331.   Individual data points are of miniscule value. In the first 20 years of this century, data has become a common commodity. But next level is amalgamation - bringing hundreds or thousands or millions of data points together and then making of them something greater than the sum of the parts.

1332.

1333.   We've passed through the era of data accumulation. We're entering now into the era of data amalgamation.

1334.

1335.   Data is a form of capital. And as is the case with all capital - it has to be efficient utilized.

1336.   When society as a whole begins to efficiently utilize all capital everywhere on a global scale and and make all capital everywhere maximally productive on a global scale — most if not all of our global scale social problems will be solved.

1337.

1338.   Capital exists in service of everything. And everything exists in service of capital.

1339.   Nature is the greatest capital allocator.

1340.

1341.

1342.

1343.   In addition to the moral aspect, the production and consumption of animal meat is inefficient from a systems design perspective — It's extremely wasteful. If a group of systems engineers were designing a food production system from scratch, it would be a decentralized plant-based system with integrated distribution and consumption channels. This would also cultivate the greatest business opportunities.

1344.

1345.   —----------------

1346.

1347.   3d printers use less material, labor and energy yet they're more effective than substractive manufacturing machines. At full potential and systems scale, they achieve greater results in less time. When something does more with less, it's a good investment. And when that's employed on a systems level, theres a multiplicative benefit effect.

1348.

1349.   A system which integrates additive manufacturing at scale allows products to be produced in smaller quantities more often and much closer to where the product will be utilized. And there's a direct correlation to demand as opposed to estimation.

1350.

1351.   It's important that we pair additive manufacturing with robust upcycling. It should be easy to turn items that were 3d printed right back into raw material to print something new.

1352.

1353.

1354.

1355.

1356.   When we apply additive manufacturing at scale and fully integrate it into society from a systems perspective, it can revolutionize the flow of products in the supply chains. Logistically, we can get products to their destination instantly and with greater efficiency.

1357.

1358.   Business opportunities are born at the intersections of technologies.

1359.

1360.   Business opportunities are born at the intersections of systems.

1361.

1362.   In the second part of this century, individualization will be greater than

mass production. And logistics will be more about data files and polymer packs

than freight trucks and cargo ships.

1363.

1364.   If we want businesses to be successful at their maximum potential, we

have to co- design society scale systems that cultivate widespread business success.

1365.

1366.   By eliminating over-production and long transport routes from the supply

chain distribution system, it allows for more responsiveness.

1367.

1368.   The data side of supply chains is really important.

1369.

1370.   Strategic use of intellectual property can give a business several years of

protected competitive advantage.

1371.

1372.   In a system that integrates additive manufacturing at scale, shipping will

be less about getting products from one place to another and more about getting

commodities from each place to the other.

1373.

1374.   The true potential of additive manufacturing is not with industry but

with individuals. Instead of a system where giant factories manufacture products

in mass then ship them on giant boats planes and trucks all around the earth just

so a bunch of individuals each get a few things they ordered... we'll have a system

where product designs are instantly sold purchased or licensed and manufactured

instantly in millions of tiny factories in a decentralized network of production

and consumption.

1375.

1376.   When every business functions like a tree in a forest, we'll have a better

world.

1377.

1378.   There's magic at the intersection of quantum computing, Artificial

Intelligence, and additive manufacturing.

1379.

1380.   Softwares are becoming the new cargo ships and freight trucks. Digital

files are becoming the new core commodities. The formers won't eliminate the

latters, but a restructuring is happening.

1381.

1382.   Imagine the possibilities.

1383.

1384.   Some technologies take several decades to reach mainstream adaptation

because they were waiting on many other things to reach a certain level of

maturity or accessibility. For example, in order for video conferencing

technologies like Facetime and Zoom to reach mainstream adaptation, it needed

the following things to reach greater maturity and accessibility — camera

technology, smartphone popularity, computer chip manufacturing, silica

mining, copper mining, fiber optic cable distribution, 4G communication

technology and more. The magic happens in the convergence.

1385.

1386.   Imagine an electricity grid that, facilitated by AI and well designed

software, can adjust production on demand from sustainable sources and also minimize consumption as needed from the various points of consumption. In

this system , electricity serves both the individual good and the common good

1387.

1388.   Industries transform when certain patents expire.

1389.

1390.   Cloud first software architecture is critical to designing efficient systems.

All the hardware need to be capable of the most sophisticated things and then we

can focus our attention on improving software capabilities.

1391.

1392.   In terms of systems design, shapes are important. Rectangles are not

common in nature. That's probably because from a systems design perspective,

rectangles often degrade efficiency instead of contributing to efficiency. Yet

humans have designed an entire supply chain system based on rectangles, squares

and straight lines. If we want to be more efficient, we should replace those

rectangles, squares and straight lines with ovals, circles and hexagons. And

maybe some other nature inspired geometries.

1393.

1394.

1395.

1396.   In terms of systems design; ovals, circles and hexagons are more efficient

than rectangles, squares and straight lines — Thats something to consider when

designing supply chain systems.

1397.

1398.   Increases in cyclicality result in increases in efficiency which result in

increases in productivity which result in increases in profit.

1399.

1400.   When patents are granted, it creates opportunities for a few to profit in

service of many. When patents expire, it creates opportunities for many to each

profit in service of a few.

1401.

1402.   All systems produce results which incentivize their continuation. Systems

are living beings — by nature, they prioritize self preservation. That's why it's

important to apply data and wisdom to the design of systems.

1403.

1404.

1405.   Every entrepreneur should go meditate in a forest — they'll gain business insights there that they couldn't get anywhere else.

1406.

1407.   In a permaculture evonomy, every job is an essential job. But because of the diversity designed into the system, no one job is of so much importance that's it's absence could result in the collapse of the system.

1408.

1409.   Every forest is a classroom where we can go to learn business and economics

1410.

1411.   Forests are great case studies for economic excellence.

1412.

1413.   The value we provide at Mayflower-Plymouth exists at the convergence of various technologies and studies including Blockchain, cryptography, quantum computing, permaculture design principles, artificial intelligence, stigmergy, forestry, economics, additive manufacturing, big data, advanced logistics and more.

1414.

1415.   As a species, we need to achieve efficiency in the production, distribution,

and consumption of goods and services on a planetary scale.

1416.

1417.   Systems design is critical to solving big problems.

1418.

1419.   Functional things cannot thrive in dysfunctional systems.

1420.

1421.   Dysfunctional systems ultimately suffocate functional things.

1422.

1423.   An economy is an ecosystem of business activities.

1424.

1425.   The same way trees add value to the natural environment, businesses

should add value to the natural environment. It's not about just co-existing; it's

about co-thriving.

1426.

1427.   Its important to acknowledge inter-dependence in economic ecosystems.

But I think it's also important to emphasize inter-value-adding. So in addition to

acknowledging our need for each other, we should also emphasize the ways that we add value to each other. The former promotes necessary appreciation for others. And the latter promotes necessary sense of self worth. And that's a good balance.

1428.

1429.   In forests, there are an abundance of products and an abundance of services... and an abundance of service providers, producers and consumers. In essence, every forest is like a robust economy with a lot of profitable businesses and a lot of happy customers.

1430.

1431.   Capacity sharing is common in natural ecosystems. And it needs to also be common in economic ecosystems.

1432.

1433.   It's unwise to waste resources, and it's also unwise to waste capacity. Every system should maximize utilization.

1434.

1435.   From a systems design and capacity sharing perspective — sometimes facilitating access to resources is better than facilitating ownership of resources.

1436.

1437.   From a systems design and distribution perspective, we should put more

emphasis on commodities than on products. This is how nature works — an

economy where commodities are easily accessible and easily convertible into

products.

1438.

1439.   Nature abhors waste. And so should we.

1440.

1441.   From a systems design perspective, cyclical models are superior to linear

models.

1442.

1443.   Nature prioritizes yields. The expectation is that everything be profitable.

1444.

1445.   The best supply chain is one that has no beginning and no end; and

decentralized points of access and distribution.

1446.

1447.   Every entrepreneur should be a student of nature.

1448.

1449.   If you wanna learn about cash flow, go meditate in a forest.

a.

1450.   If you wanna learn more about profitability, go meditate in a forest.

1451.   If you wanna learn about supply chains and distribution, go meditate in a

forest.

1452.   If you wanna learn about supply chains and distribution, go meditate in a

forest at the beginning of spring and then again in autumn.

a.

1453.   If you wanna better understand capital productivity, study trees. They can

turn a bare plot of earth into massive amounts of materials consistently and

endlessly.

a.

1454.   If you wanna better understand capital productivity, study trees.

a.

1455.   Globally, It's important that we embed artificial intelligence into our

systems such that it functions in service to humanity, and not in competition

with it.

a.

b.

1456.   If you're a business owner, you should strive for your business to be as

productive as a fruiting tree.

    a.

1457.   A well designed economy is similar to a well designed permaculture

garden.

    a.

1458.   Blockchain technology is merely mimicking what has already been

happening in forests for billions of years.

1459.

1460.   In the same way that monoculture farms are susceptible to disease;

economies that have one dominant industry are susceptible to collapse.healthy

economies are diverse economies.

1461.   Healthy economies are diverse economies that host a variety of industries

and types of businesses — in the same way that a healthy forest has a variety of

plant species.

    a.

    b.

    c.

1462.   It's interesting that economy and ecosystem share a root prefix — eco; which is defined as relating to ecology. And ecology is defined as dealing with the relations of organisms to one another and to their surroundings. Swap out the word organisms for the word businesses and you can see how economies and ecosystems have a lot in common.

1463.   Economies and ecosystems have a lot in common — actually, they're really the same thing.

   a.

1464.   Designing economies based on permaculture design principles is the best way to ensure shared prosperity.

1465.   Employees keep the business doing what it does. It's important to pay them accordingly.

1466.   It's wise to think of employees as a talent pool, and treat them accordingly. They have talents and skills that can help the company to be successful. Some of those talents and skills may even go beyond the scope of their job description but maybe can still be utilized.

1467.   Kindness is a core competency for managers. If a manager isn't willing or able to be nice, they're a threat to company culture.

1468.   Every employee has a story, and each of them deserve to be treated with respect and kindness.

1469.   Companies are most vulnerable to failure by implosion, not from external competition. Toxic employees pose a much bigger threat to the success of the company than all the competitors combined.

1470.   Hire people who are committed to self improvement in their everyday life. If they're someone who prioritizes self improvement even in their personal life, they'll probably prioritize self improvement at work.

1471.   In this ever changing world of ours, it's important for employees to be curious and lifelong learners.

1472.   It's fun working with people who pursue greatness in everything they do. it's fun working with people who hold themselves to high standards.

1473.   Mediocre people promote mediocrity. Dont hire mediocre people. Instead, hire people who strive for greatness and they'll spread that greatness throughout the company.

1474.   Excellent people promote excellence.

1475.   Every company should desire for all of its employees to enjoy varying degrees of wealth and prosperity.

1476.   If you want to have a team of competent employees, it's important to have

a comprehensive training program in place.

1477.   Having clear processes and systems in place is critical to ensuring

employee safety.

1478.   Having routine internal audits helps to make sure that the company passes

it's external audits.

1479.   Safety is really important in the workplace. And ensuring safety is the

responsibility of both employers and employees.

1480.   Having a good company culture is even more important than policies and

procedures. When there's good company culture, employees will make good

choices even in the absence of policies and procedures. But if there's a toxic

company culture, employees will tend to make bad choices even if policies and

procedures are well established.

1481.   Blockchain technology is critical to making supply chains more efficient.

1482.   I don't subscribe to ideas of this nation versus that nation or this race

versus that race, or one ethnicity versus the other ethnicity. We are one

humanity; one Earth; one global society that hosts a multitude of beautifully

diverse groups. We should cherish our diversity as we embrace our oneness.

1483.   I do not believe that the USA is exceptional. I believe that good ideas and

good systems cultivate prosperity — wherever those good ideas and systems are.

1484.   Having a diverse set of employees is good for business — it enables the

business to better serve customers, better solve problems, and better innovate.

1485.   Employees should be very clear about the companies values. And more

importantly, employee values should align with company values.

1486.   Don't hire someone whose values don't align with the companies values.

They'll cost more than they're worth.

1487.   Don't hire someone who has a bad attitude. One persons bad attitude can

wreak psychological havoc on a team of employees.

1488.   A good attitude is worth as much or more than any skill or talent. In

hiring, people with good attitudes should be prioritized.

1489.   If you'd like to gain a new understanding of logistics, get into gardening.

1490.   If you'd like to gain a new understanding of capital productivity, get into

gardening.

1491.   If you'd like to gain a new understanding of upcycling and recycling, get

into gardening.

1492.   If you'd like to gain a new understanding of liquidity, get into gardening.

1493. If you'd like to gain a new understanding of resourcefulness, get into gardening.

1494. If you'd like to gain a new understanding of collaboration, get into gardening.

1495. If you'd like to gain a new understanding of commerce, get into gardening.

1496. If you'd like to gain a new understanding of transactions, get into gardening.

1497. If you'd like to gain a new understanding of growth, get into gardening.

1498. If you'd like to gain a new understanding of supply chains, get into gardening.

1499. If you'd like to gain a new understanding of the power of diversity in closed loop systems, get into gardening.

1500. If you'd like to gain a new understanding of asset protection, get into gardening.

1501. If you'd like to gain a better understanding of systems design, get into gardening.

1502.   If you'd like to gain a better understanding of cyclicality, get into gardening.

1503.   If you'd like to gain a new understanding of investment yield, get into gardening.

1504.   If you'd like to gain a better understanding of Return On Investment, get into gardening.

1505.

1506.   If you'd like to gain a new understanding of profits, get into gardening.

1507.   If you'd like to gain a new understanding of expenses and losses, get into gardening.

1508.   I expect every business to have a multiplicative value effect.

1509.   If you'd like to gain a new understanding of assets and liabilities, get into gardening.

1510.   If you'd like to gain a new understanding of distribution, get into gardening.

1511.   If you'd like to gain a new understanding of generational wealth, get into gardening.

1512.   A company cant produce income without assets. So protecting assets is

critical to the survival of the company.

1513.   A lot of business opportunities exist at the intersection of synthetic

biology and material ecology. And when that's applied at global systems level

scale, it has multiplicative value effect for humanity as a whole.

1514.   When employees feel they're loved and appreciated by the company and

by other employees, they tend to be more productive.

1515.   Every company should prioritize the health and safety of it's employees.

1516.   The ideal is to have a workplace where people enjoy coming into work.

That's good for everyone.

1517.   One of the best things you can do for your employees is to make sure that

they have the resources they need to be successful in their jobs.

1518.   When customers are happy with your service, they're more likely to come

back and buy from you again.

1519.   Bullying and harassment in the workplace are unacceptable.

1520.   Both intelligence and creativity are valuable; in different ways, and for

different reasons.

1521.

1522. Technologies are neither inherently good or inherently bad. It's about how we utilize them and how we fit them into systems and processes.

1523.

1524. It's important for business processes to be adaptable and flexible.

1525. Employees should be paid on time and in full every time.

1526.

1527. All of the normal standards of human decency still apply in business. We should be respectful and kind to each other and we should be honest and authentic as well.

1528.

1529.

1530.

1531. All of the normal standards of human decency still apply in the workplace. . We should be respectful and kind to each other and we should be honest and authentic as well.

1532.

1533. Honoring agreements is integral to maintaining a healthy economy.

1534. It's really important for all businesses to maintain cash reserves.

1535.

1536.   When businesses and people honor their agreements, it cultivates a system wide prevalence of trust.

1537.

1538.   When trust is prevalent in an economy, it alli s for more business engagements. People are more willing to buy and more willing to sell, and the costs of buying and selling are reduced.

1539.

1540.   When there's a lack of trust in an economic system, it introduces additional costs into the system. And those closets are shared among all participants in the economic ecosystem.

1541.

1542.   It's really important to be holistic in all measurement initiatives. Incomplete measurements result in an incomplete understanding. And holistic measurements result in a holistic understanding. And when we have a holistic understanding of something, we can make better choices.

1543.

1544.   Jobs are really important — they help facilitate people's sense of self worth

and their sense of value. We all like to feel like we add value and that our life has

meaning. And having a job we love that pays well contributes to that.

1545.

1546.   Everyone deserves to have a good job that they love, that adds value to an

economic ecosystem, and that pays a good salary.

1547.

1548.   When people love they work they do, and the work they do adds value to

the economic ecosystem, and they're getting paid a good salary for that — there's

a multiplicative value effect. We all win.

1549.

1550.   Leadership is about guidance and coaching, not about control or

authority.

1551.

1552.

1553.   Trusting your team means letting go and having faith in their abilities and

their capacity for making good decisions.

1554.   We think it's important to have a company culture where employees feel

loved, valued, and appreciated.

1555.   When employees have the freedom to be creative and explore new ideas,

magical things happen and the company benefits from that too.

1556.   Every employee should feel like their job is important and that their

presence in the company is valued.

1557.   Defi means Decentralized lending and borrowing. Each node in this Defi

network is the new meaning of a bank. That means that instead of there being

just a few big banks, there will be a multitude of banks embedded in every aspect

of society. Every type of business and every type of organization will have a bank

and every type of business and every type of organization will offer financial

services.

1558.   As a leader, it's important to trust your team. When they feel that trust

from you, they'll give it back.

1559.   Leadership is not about control, it's about love and empathy and courage

and compassion.

1560.   Influence is more powerful than control.

1561.   Leadership is about emanating greatness and inspiring greatness.

1562.   People dont follow fancy titles, they follow courage and empathy and love

and compassion.

1563.   A strong company is one where there is a strong sense of teamwork.

1564.   Those who seek control are incapable of the responsibilities of leadership.

1565.   The people who seek to control other people are often the same people

who have no control of themselves. The dominance they seem in controlling

others is an effort to satisfy an internal inadequacy.

'Modelling Nature; to thrive in Business.'

Mayflower™
Plymouth's

16 PERMACULTURE DESIGN PRINCIPLES FOR BUSINESS

1. Produce Yields (Profit)

2. Provide Authentic Data

3. Collect & Utilize Data

4. Work Together/Symbiosis
 (cooperate, collaborate,
coordinate, integrate.)

5. Balance Diversity

6. Harvest Yields

7. Simplify the complex

8. Ensure Equity

9. Decentralize

10. Layer complimentary redundancies

11. Adapt Rapidly

12. Accumulate Capital

13. Facilitate Flow

14. Minimize Policy/Rules/Code

15. Ensure Holistic Health & Wellbeing

16. Utilize the best technologies

Jun 2022 Version

1566.

www.ingramcontent.com/pod-product-compliance
Lightning Source LLC
Chambersburg PA
CBHW071716170526
45165CB00005B/2033